WATERGATE AND THE LAW

WATERGATE AND THE LAW

Political Campaigns and Presidential Power

Ralph K. Winter, Jr.

American Enterprise Institute for Public Policy Research
Washington, D. C.

250445

Domestic Affairs Study 22, March 1974
Second printing, August 1974
ISBN 0-8447-3124-2

Library of Congress Catalog Card No. L. C. 74-77263

Printed in the United States of America

PREFACE

Senator Sam J. Ervin, Jr., and Senator Howard H. Baker, Jr., on behalf of the Senate Select Committee on Presidential Campaign Activities, requested the American Enterprise Institute and several other organizations to aid the committee in identifying the legislative implications of the facts developed during the recent Watergate hearings. In particular, the committee requested a report on "the options or alternatives that might feasibly be open for serious contemplation by the committee" and the advantages and disadvantages of each option.

Pursuant to this request, AEI commissioned a study of the legislative implications of the Watergate hearings and named a panel of distinguished scholars to serve as consultants. The fruits of this undertaking include the present report by the project director, Professor Ralph K. Winter, Jr., as well as two AEI Round Tables in which members of the project's advisory panel will discuss the report. These discussions will be videotaped for television and subsequently published. The project was supported in part by a grant from the Ford Foundation.

The views expressed in the report are those of the author and do not necessarily reflect the views of the members of the advisory panel or of the staff, officers or trustees of AEI.

Joseph G. Butts
Director of Legislative Analysis
American Enterprise Institute
for Public Policy Research

CONTENTS

But the Judge said he never had summed up before;
So the Snark undertook it instead,
And summed it so well that it came to far more
Than the Witnesses ever had said!

Lewis Carroll
The Hunting of the Snark:
The Barrister's Dream

INTRODUCTION

An affair as spectacular as Watergate is bound to leave in its wake legislative opportunities that might otherwise not exist. This would be the case even if the American inclination to resort to law as a solution to every political and social blemish were not a prominent national characteristic. But a national characteristic it is, and the observer who dares suggest that existing legal and institutional arrangements are for the most part adequate is likely to be viewed as a hopeless apologist for the corruption of the American political process.

The existence of great pressure to do something cannot, however, wholly drown out the anxious cry—"but do what?" After the short-run questions of individual criminality and presidential impeachment are faced, there remains cause to puzzle over what can be done to strengthen the resistance of the American political system to such trauma.

Watergate is a poor vehicle for addressing questions of major reform. Although so spectacular a scandal seems naturally to generate the conviction that the American legal system has gone fundamentally awry, even cursory reflection reveals that it is the vicissitudes of crime detection that have provided the drama of Watergate—not the failure of substantive law. A headlong rush into substantive reform may be exactly the wrong response. The investigation of the Senate Select Committee on Presidential Campaign Activities has focused hardly at all on the relationship of American legal and institutional arrangements to the disclosures. Instead, the hearings were almost entirely obsessed with questions of individual guilt or innocence. Finally, because the Senate limited the committee's jurisdiction to the 1972 election,[1] it has been difficult to judge the extent to which the activities disclosed are standard or aberrational.

Watergate may thus be history less in danger of being ignored than misunderstood. Few would be willing to defend the universality of Mr. Justice Holmes's proposition that "great cases like hard cases make bad law."[2] Few would also, however, challenge the existence of the real danger which underlies the dictum, the danger that extraordinary events provide a shaky foundation for enduring legal and institutional arrangements. The power to fix attention is the power to distract from all else, and a policy maker who focuses solely on Watergate may be like a landscape artist who observes his subject only at close range with a microscope.

For example, investigation of Watergate revealed that Mr. L. Patrick Gray had burned files he had come to possess in his capacity as acting director of the Federal Bureau of Investigation (FBI). Although Mr. Gray attributed the burning to considerations of national security, the material was potentially such an embarrassment to the administration that Messrs. Ehrlichman and Dean had left him with no doubt of their desire that it be destroyed.[3] Mr. Gray further

---

[1] The Senate Select Committee on Presidential Campaign Activities was established by Senate Resolution 60, 93rd Congress, 1st session, adopted unanimously by the Senate on February 7, 1973. The text of the resolution is reprinted in *Hearings before the Select Committee on Presidential Campaign Activities of the United States Senate*, 93rd Congress, 1st session (1973), Phase I: Watergate Investigation, Book 1, p. 427 (hereinafter referred to as *Select Committee Hearings*).

[2] Holmes, J. (dissenting) in Northern Securities Company v. United States, 193 U.S. 197, 400 (1904).

[3] Testimony of Louis Patrick Gray, III, former acting director, Federal Bureau of Investigation, in *Select Committee Hearings* (mimeo.), vol. 35, pp. 7072-7084, particularly the statement at pp. 7072-7073:

"After the usual greetings were exchanged, Mr. Ehrlichman said something very close to, 'John has something that he wants to turn over to you.' I then noticed that Mr. Dean had in his hands two white manila legal size file folders. It is my recollection that these folders were not in envelopes at this time.

"Mr. Dean then told me that these files contained copies of sensitive and classified papers of a political nature that Howard Hunt had been working on. He said that they have national security implications or overtones, have absolutely nothing to do with Watergate and have no bearing on the Watergate investigation whatsoever. Either Mr. Dean or Mr. Ehrlichman said that these files should not be allowed to confuse or muddy the issues in the Watergate case.

"I asked whether these files should become a part of our FBI Watergate file. Mr. Dean said these should not become a part of our FBI Watergate file, but that he wanted to be able to say, if called upon later, that he had turned all of Howard Hunt's files over to the FBI.

"I distinctly recall Mr. Dean saying that these files were 'political dynamite,' and 'clearly should not see the light of day.'

revealed that he believed it his duty to respond to requests from the counsel to the President (Mr. Dean) even though the requests plainly did not come through his chain of command, that is, Mr. Gray's immediate superior, the attorney general of the United States.[4]

One might conclude from this that arrangements to increase the FBI's independence from political control are needed. Indeed, such claims are now being made.

There is more than a little irony in these claims, inasmuch as exactly the opposite conclusion was drawn in the recent past as a result of the behavior of Mr. Gray's predecessor. The conventional wisdom of 1971 was that Mr. J. Edgar Hoover had achieved for the FBI too much independence from elected officials and was thus able to thwart the Kennedy administration in its attempts to reorder the agency's priorities.[5]

Watergate must not be treated as a burst of divine inspiration, but as an incident with incremental lessons, lessons to be mastered only in a historical perspective. There are no automatic legislative responses to be made, and each proposal must be judged on its overall merits rather than on some instant demonstration of validity allegedly found in the record of the Select Committee.

Cries for reform in the wake of Watergate are of two sorts. The first sort asserts that the affair shows the inadequacy of our laws regulating political campaigns, in particular the inadequacy of laws on campaign financing [6] and on surreptitious or illegal tactics—in the lexicon of the Select Committee, "dirty tricks." The second attributes the affair to the "unwarranted and unprecedented expan-

---

(Footnote 3 continued)

"It is true that neither Mr. Ehrlichman nor Mr. Dean expressly instructed me to destroy the files. But there was, and is, no doubt in my mind that destruction was intended. Neither Mr. Dean nor Mr. Ehrlichman said or implied that I was being given the documents personally merely to safeguard against leaks. As I believe each of them has testified before this committee the White House regarded the FBI as a source of leaks. The clear implication of the substance and tone of their remarks was that these two files were to be destroyed and I interpreted this to be an order from the counsel to the President of the United States issued in the presence of one of the two top assistants to the President of the United States."

[4] Ibid., vol. 36 (mimeo.), p. 7111 ff.

[5] See, for example, Victor S. Navasky, *Kennedy Justice* (New York: Atheneum, 1971), Chapter 3, "Civil Rights: The Movement and the General," pp. 96-155.

[6] See, for example, testimony of Senator Kennedy, reprinted in *Congressional Record*, November 15, 1973, p. S 20449.

sion of presidential power"[7] and calls for measures curtailing the powers of the President.

The statement of these issues should underscore the danger of focusing solely on Watergate. They are not, after all, new to the American political scene but have given rise to a vast literature over the years. This literature at the very least demonstrated the risk of bringing about major changes in the political process as a result of a single spectacular incident. History teaches that one's view of these issues is exceedingly difficult to separate from one's immediate and partisan political objectives. The *New York Times*, for example, treated the campaign reform legislation of 1971 as a high-priority item. Yet when that legislation prevented political advertising by the American Civil Liberties Union just a few months later, the *Times's* lawyers were in court charging that it was "shot through with constitutional deficiencies."[8] And the zeal of some scholars in defending the constitutional authority of Presidents Roosevelt and Truman often seems to have been exceeded only by their zeal in condemning the exercise of it by President Nixon.[9] Whatever the merits of these partisan political objectives, they count for naught where the issue is legislative reform. In this proposition, it would seem, all fair-minded men must agree.

---

[7] Arthur M. Schlesinger, Jr., *The Imperial Presidency* (Boston: Houghton-Mifflin Co., 1973), p. 275.

[8] Brief for *New York Times* as amicus curiae, p. 16, American Civil Liberties Union v. Jennings, Civil No. 1967-72 (D.D.C., 1972).

[9] See generally, Arthur M. Schlesinger, Jr., *The Imperial Presidency*.

1
WATERGATE AND THE REGULATION OF POLITICAL CAMPAIGNS

Campaign Financing

The principal measures proposed in the wake of Watergate are relatively old and deceptively simple. In general outline they include a subsidy from public funds for candidates for federal office—a subsidy that would pay all or part of the candidates' campaign costs.[1] This subsidy would be complemented (1) by legal limits on the amount spent by a candidate or those furthering a candidacy and (2) by legal limits on the size of individual financial contributions to a candidate or (3) by the outlawing of all private financing.

These proposals are of critical importance. If adopted, they will alter the political process and will have results transcending the issue of campaign financing. And because they regulate campaign advocacy, they may interfere with freedom of expression and ought not be implemented without searching consideration. When scrutinized, however, the proposals lack a foundation in established scholarship and ignore the grave dangers that such regulation threatens for a free society.

This can be demonstrated by viewing private campaign financing from three perspectives: (1) in terms of the available evidence on its impact on the American political process, (2) in terms of its positive functions, and (3) as a problem in legal regulation.

Private Campaign Financing: The Available Evidence. If the rhetoric employed by the opponents of private campaign financing is valid, there can be no doubt in anyone's mind that its influence ought to be

---

[1] See, for example, S. 1103, 93rd Congress, 1st session (1973); hereinafter referred to as the Hart bill, after its author, Senator Hart.

5

eliminated. "There is nothing," we are told, ". . . that creates more mischief, more corruption and more alienation and distrust. . . ." [2] One prominent senator has gone so far as to state that "most, and probably all, of the serious problems facing this country today have their roots in the way we finance political campaigns. . . ." [3]

No one denies that elections are expensive, but the importance of campaign money is usually exaggerated by the opponents of private financing. Partly this is because the campaign period itself is overrated. Because it is a highly visible and concentrated period of excitement and action, we tend to attribute far more importance to campaigns than they deserve. Studies have shown that the shifts of public opinion which affect elections most decisively usually take place between campaigns, rather than during them. [4] In the vast

---

[2] Statement of John W. Gardner, *Hearings on S. 372 before the Subcommittee on Communications of the Committee on Commerce, United States Senate*, 93rd Congress, 1st session (1973), p. 61 and p. 90 (hereinafter referred to as *Hearings on S. 372*).

[3] See note 6, Introduction, *supra*.

[4] What common observation suggests, scholarly study confirms. Consider the conclusions the noted V. O. Key reached:

". . . . One way to narrow the problem of estimating the effects of campaigns is to examine, first, other factors that perhaps have greater weight in determining the outcome of elections than campaigns themselves. One of these factors is the traditional or consistent vote. It is apparent that a large proportion of the electorate votes for the party in one election that it supported in the preceding election. These diehard partisans are seemingly untouched by the events of the campaign. Around four-fifths of the voters may ordinarily be placed in the category of loyal partisans. . . .

"Another point that aids in getting down to the effects of campaigns is this: Changes in party loyalties and voting intentions occur all during the four-year period of a President's incumbency. The trend of opinion may be such that the changes in voting intentions during the more than three years before the campaign proper begins may exceed the changes occurring during the period of intensive campaigning. The 'propaganda of events' or the 'propaganda of deeds' may make or lose more votes than all that is said during the course of the campaign. . . .

"Some evidence is available to support the assertion that long-term trends of sentiment may be more efficacious in altering voting intentions than campaign oratory. . . .

". . . . Lazarsfeld suggests that campaigns may have three principal effects: reinforcement, activation, and conversion. The reinforcement effect consists simply in the fact that the events of the campaign reinforce the voting intentions and party loyalties of the diehard partisans. . . .

"The activation effect of campaigns consists in the arousing of persons indifferent at the outset and inducing them to vote. In considerable measure those whose disinterest is turned into an inclination to vote are persuaded to vote in the manner in which one would have predicted on the basis of their personal characteristics. . . .

majority of elections, the campaign in fact has little or no effect. This is so even in contests for the presidency, contests which involve large, well-organized and visible campaigns. In only three of the last eleven elections can it even be said that the campaign *may* have affected the outcome.[5] In congressional races, the role of the campaign diminishes further. While the impact of campaign money on elections would never seem to exceed the impact of the campaign itself, the point must be qualified by the fact that politicians may misperceive the relative insignificance of campaigns and attribute more importance to campaign money than is justified. If so, its influence will accord with that perception.

Although the escalating campaign costs of recent years are widely pointed to, we do not really know how much was spent before television when campaign expenditures were not readily observable. Even now, the estimated amount spent for all elective offices in 1972, national, state and local, was less than was spent in that year by each of two companies on their commercial advertising.[6]

Still, campaigns are costly, and large contributions seem an easy way to gain favor. The Watergate hearings reveal that potential

---

(Footnote 4 continued)

"Very few people are converted by a campaign, that is, change their voting intentions between the time of the beginning of the campaign and the election itself. . . .

"The state of research on the effects of campaigns, let it be repeated, is such that only limited conclusions may be drawn. Yet the available studies and common observation suggest that campaigns mainly renew the loyalties of the faithful, bring the apathetic out to the polls for the expression of their predispositions, and effect the conversion of a very few electors." (V. O. Key, Jr., *Politics, Parties and Pressure Groups* (New York: T. Y. Crowell, 1947), pp. 447-449).

Others have similarly concluded:

"The campaign period, then, would seem inherently to be less a period of potential change than a period of political entrenchment, a period in which prior attitudes are reaffirmed. This may well be a real paradox of political life: We are accustomed to think of campaign periods as the dynamic times when political passions are aroused and wholesale changeover results, and of periods between as the quiescent years, when people tend to forget about politics and are less attentive to the larger political environment. Yet changes in political opinion and in the general political climate may be less characteristic of the days of arousal than of the 'quiescent' times between campaigns." (K. and G. Lang, "The Mass Media and Voting," in *American Voting Behavior*, Eugene Burdick and Arthur Brodbeck, eds. (New York: Free Press, 1959), p. 219).

[5] These would be the election campaigns of 1948, 1960 and 1968. Interestingly, in the campaigns of 1948 and 1968, there were significant third (and in the 1948 case, fourth) party efforts mounted. In none of the eight elections where campaigns appeared not to affect the outcome were there major third party candidates.

[6] Statement of Herbert E. Alexander in *Hearings on S. 372*, p. 219.

donors may be reminded of their dependence on governmental decisions by public officials or their representatives.[7] Some individuals give seemingly inordinate amounts. Finally, continued allegations of improper influence have eroded confidence in the political process.

Given all this, the case for regulation should not be summarily dismissed, and the roles played by private campaign money must be carefully weighed. Certain functions are clearly undesirable. Some contributors doubtless make contributions in the hope of obtaining personal favors ranging from the trivial (dinner invitations) to the malevolent. Awarding ambassadorships in return for large contributions may not be the most desirable method of choosing American representatives abroad. To exercise administrative discretion in favor of large political contributors, as in awarding government contracts, is not only undesirable but in most cases illegal. Where the contribution follows a pointed reminder from a public official, governmental power is clearly being misused.

That some abuses exist, however, does not justify the conclusions reached by the opponents of private campaign financing. The abuses may be far more isolated than would appear from the sensationalized way in which they are exposed. Horror stories are effective because they horrify, not because they illuminate. Moreover, the abuses may (in fact, do) yield to remedies considerably narrower than the proposals now being made.[8]

Where the candidacies of the rich are concerned, the allegations about wealth doubtless contain some truth but their import is inconclusive. If wealth alone determined election results, one would have to conclude that the political careers of Nelson Rockefeller and the Kennedys were illegitimate. Obviously, their political success is based on more than wealth. The allegations also fail to demonstrate overall harm to the system. Admittedly, personal wealth aids a candidate in a way that seems unfair. But if the influence of campaign money were eliminated, even more irrational factors (as, for example, the media exposure which falls to astronauts, athletes and sportscasters) might become more significant. Moreover, there is no evidence that the political behavior of officeholders with personal wealth differs greatly from that of those without.

In any event, the expectation that limiting or abolishing the use of private campaign money will somehow "equalize" rich and poor aspirants to office seems unrealistic. *The real advantage of*

---

[7] See generally, for example, testimony of Claude C. Wild, Jr., *Select Committee Hearings* (mimeo.), pp. 10023-10079.

[8] See p. 23, infra.

wealthy political aspirants is the free time they can devote to politics or to public service related to politics. Permitting the raising and expending of private money by less affluent candidates may thus be more of an "equalizer" than prohibiting it.

The available evidence does not support the view that money is more than one of a number of factors affecting the electoral process or that it exclusively supports a narrow range of ideas on public policy. No one seriously contends that money has been decisive in presidential elections.[9] Of course, candidates of third parties raise less money than candidates of major parties, but that is because of their anticipated weakness at the polls and not because fringe movements are unable to raise funds. History furnishes a number of movements which began at the fringe and which, because they raised salient issues, were able to attract funds and, over time, affect the

---

[9] The Democratic Party, for instance, elected Presidents from 1932 to 1952, but spent less money than the Republicans. In more recent years, John Kennedy spent his party into debt in 1960, but that may well have been necessary to overcome what was at that time a religious disability. As one scholar computed 1960 spending, "the 1960 ratio of Democratic to Republican spending appears to have been almost as close as the 1960 election returns." See Herbert E. Alexander, *Financing the 1960 Election* (Princeton, N. J.: Citizens' Research Foundation, 1961), pp. 9-11. In 1964 Barry Goldwater considerably broadened the Republican Party's financial base and outspent his Democratic opponent. Nevertheless, the best-financed and most narrowly based Democratic campaign in history to that point, plus the advantages of incumbency, more than outweighed Goldwater's mass contributions. See Alexander, *Financing the 1964 Election* (Princeton, N. J.: Citizens' Research Foundation, 1966), pp. 7-17. The Goldwater campaign (and, to a lesser extent, the McGovern campaign) demonstrate an interesting interrelationship of two themes in the text: (1) campaign money tends to go to winners, and (2) intensely held feelings generate funds supporting those feelings. Although Goldwater and McGovern consistently showed poorly in the public opinion polls, the strong philosophical convictions of their supporters nonetheless generated considerable amounts of money, especially in relatively small donations. The Nixon 1972 victory repeated the 1960 pattern: contributions mirrored almost exactly the eventual popular vote totals of the two major candidates. Although both Goldwater and McGovern were swamped on election day, they at least had an opportunity to voice the strongly held feelings of their ardent supporters. That they did so against strongly entrenched incumbent Presidents and that two men of such differing political persuasions could become nominees of the two major parties only eight years apart is an amazing testimony to the freedom of American politics. The only apparent exception to the proposition in the text accompanying this footnote is the 1968 election. Republicans outspent Democrats in the general election campaign, but the Democrats exceeded Republican outlays in the pre-conventions struggles for the nomination. The political reality of 1968 thus explains the Democrats' inability to raise money: the party began in debt and was deeply and acrimoniously split; it ended in even greater debt and with internal turmoil still unresolved. Alexander, *Financing the 1968 Election* (Indianapolis: D. C. Heath & Co., 1969).

course of American history. Consider the achievements of the National Association for the Advancement of Colored People (NAACP). Once such movements take hold, candidates representing their points of view get campaign money.

The role of the rich patron in bringing about change should not be ignored. As Milton Friedman has noted:

> Radical movements . . . have typically been supported by a few wealthy individuals who have become persuaded— by a Frederick Vanderbilt Field, or an Anita McCormick Blaine, or a Corliss Lamont, to mention a few names recently prominent, or by a Friedrich Engels, to go further back. This is a role of inequality of wealth in preserving political freedom that is seldom noted—the role of the patron.[10]

The allegations that money blocks social change quite simply ignore history. During the last forty years, an immense amount of social and regulatory legislation has been enacted. This alone would refute the assertion that campaign money is a barrier to change.[11]

Of course, contributions sometimes play an undesirable or even corrupting role. But no system is without friction and, where the system involves money, whether it be taxation, welfare, or campaign contributions, there will be abuses. Contrary to the views so widely expressed, however, serious scholars generally agree that money is only one factor influencing elections and that its impact is not, on balance, either decisive or harmful.

For example, in response to the rhetorical question, "Does money win?" Dr. Herbert E. Alexander of the Citizens' Research Foundation answered that money is the "common denominator helping to shape the factors that make for electoral success. . . ."[12] He agreed that certain minimal amounts are probably necessary, but noted that "little is known of the marginal increment per dollar or of the differential effectiveness of the various campaign techniques."[13] Among other

---

[10] Milton Friedman, *Capitalism and Freedom* (Chicago: University of Chicago Press, 1962), p. 17.

[11] The inconclusive results of the social programs of the 1960s may be a cause of the present flap over campaign financing. Frustrated over the failure of these programs to produce the expected results, their proponents may automatically assume that something must be wrong with the political process.

[12] Herbert E. Alexander, "Links and Contrasts Among American Parties and Party Subsystems," in *Comparative Political Finance: The Financing of Party Organizations and Election Campaigns*, Arnold J. Heidenheimer, ed. (Indianapolis: D. C. Heath & Co., 1970), p. 104.

[13] Ibid., p. 103.

possibly determining factors, Alexander listed the predisposition of voters, the issues, group support, incumbency, chances for electoral victory, sympathy on the part of the mass media, and a collection of other factors (religion, divorce, and color).[14] On another occasion, Dr. Alexander testified:

> . . . it is well to remember that the availability of money for a given campaign may be an inherent effect of our democratic and pluralistic system—either the constitutional right to spend one's own money or to financially support candidates with congenial viewpoints or a manifestation of popularity. This is not to say that monied interests do not sometimes take advantage of a candidate's need for funds, or that candidates do not sometimes become beholden to special interests. They do, but that is part of the price we pay for a democratic system in which political party discipline is lacking and the candidate (and some of the public) may value his independence from the party.[15]

David Adamany reached essentially the same conclusions when he argued that "primarily, the patterns of campaign finance are a response to the political environment; but it is also true that the relationship is reciprocal inasmuch as the uses of money may, within very significant limits, shape the political system."[16] The programmatic orientation of parties and candidates is the resource Adamany deems most important, followed by personal charisma, finance organization, incumbency, and several others.[17] Unlike many of the reform advocates, he believes that:

> . . . a sophisticated examination shows that by most measures Americans pay a small cost for the maintenance of an adversary political process in a complicated federal system with its many elective offices at a variety of levels of government.
>
> . . . Even the scholarly work on campaign finance tends to concentrate on the amounts spent, the sources from which the money is raised, and the uses to which the money is put. These data are all helpful, but they do not show the relationship of campaign finance to the political environment— to the kinds of party systems, the available channels of

---

[14] Ibid., pp. 103-104.

[15] Statement of Dr. Herbert E. Alexander in *Hearings on S. 372*, p. 224.

[16] David Adamany, *Financing Politics: Recent Wisconsin Elections* (Madison: University of Wisconsin Press, 1969), p. 230.

[17] Ibid., pp. 231-233.

communication, and other political and social phenomena. Nor is money ordinarily viewed as a form of functional representation by groups in the community and as just one of the several ways in which groups may seek their policy objectives through the allocation of resources to the political process.

. . . Yet much less attention is given to money as a form of functional representation than to the very infrequent instances in which campaign gifts are made for the purpose of procuring actions by public officials which would not have been forthcoming in the absence of contributions.[18]

Alexander Heard, in his classic work on campaign finance, *The Costs of Democracy*, concluded:

And it has been repeatedly demonstrated he who pays the piper does *not* always call the tune, at least not in politics. Politicians prize votes more than dollars.

Contrary to frequent assertions, American campaign monies are *not* supplied solely by a small handful of fat cats. Many millions of people now give to politics. Even those who give several hundred dollars each number in the tens of thousands.

And the traditional fat cats are *not* all of one species, allied against common adversaries. Big givers show up importantly in both parties and on behalf of many opposing candidates.[19]

In their work, *Presidential Elections*, Professors Nelson Polsby and Aaron Wildavsky wrote:

It is exceedingly difficult to get reliable information on an event that involves a decision *not* to act. Such an event would be a decision by a political candidate not to run because he could not raise the money. There is, of course, no literature on this subject. But there have undoubtedly been some men whose inability to raise the cash has proven fatal to their chance of being considered for the nomination. While this is most regrettable, a more important question concerns whether there has been systematic bias in favor of or against certain kinds of men that consistently alters the outcome of Presidential nominations. We can immediately dismiss the notion that the richest man automatically comes out on top. If that were the case, Rockefeller would have

---

[18] Ibid., p. 244.

[19] Alexander Heard, *The Costs of Democracy* (Chapel Hill: University of North Carolina Press, 1960), p. 6.

triumphed over Goldwater, Taft over Eisenhower, and neither Nixon nor Stevenson would have been nominated.

The ability to raise money is not only a matter of personal wealth but of being able to attract funds from others. Does this mean that only candidates attractive to the wealthy can run? It might be said that the problem is not so much whether it helps to be rich but whether men who favor the causes of the rich have the advantage over those who favor the poor. There is little evidence to support such a view. Given the nature of the American electorate, no candidate would openly admit to being the candidate only of the rich. Candidates holding a variety of views on economic issues—most of which are highly technical—manage to run for the nominations of both parties. If candidates are generally chosen from among men who differ but little on most substantive issues the reason is not because the rich are withholding their money from more radical candidates but rather because the distribution of opinions in the electorate renders the cause of such men hopeless. Our conclusion is that it is nice to be rich; some men who lack funds may be disadvantaged. From the standpoint of the total political system, however, the nomination process does not appear to bar types of men who are otherwise acceptable to the electorate.

Although the difference in ability of the two parties to raise money is not in any sense a critical determinant of national elections, large sums of money are necessary to run campaigns. May not those who contribute or raise money in large amounts thereby gain influence not available to others? Aware that the answer to this question is not a simple one, we would say, "Yes, but not overly much." What contributors or fund raisers (the financial middlemen) get to begin with is access to centers of decision-making. Control over money certainly makes it easier to get in and present one's case. Men of wealth, however, are likely to have substantial economic interests which would provide them with good access whether or not they made contributions. If no significant interest feels disadvantaged by what these contributors want, they may well be given the benefit of the doubt. But in matters of great moment, where the varied interests in our society are in contention, it is doubtful whether control over money goes very far with a President.[20]

[20] Nelson W. Polsby and Aaron B. Wildavsky, *Presidential Elections: Strategies of American Electoral Politics*, 2d ed. (New York: Charles Scribner's Sons, 1968), pp. 39-40.

Finally, the much respected political scientist, the late V. O. Key, noted:

> Considerable analysis has been made of the sources of contributions to national committees. The findings, in essence, seem to be that each party draws heavily on those elements traditionally associated with it. . . . The cynical view that a campaign contribution is equivalent to a bribe at times indubitably matches the facts. Yet the significance of money in politics can be grasped only by a view that places party finance in the total context of the political process. . . . That the unbridled dominance of money would run counter to the tenets of a democratic order may be indisputable. On the other hand, a democratic regime that tyrannized men of wealth would both commit injustice and perhaps destroy its instruments of production.[21]

Matched against this array of respected scholarship is little more than the impressionistic assertion that some kind of "correlation" exists between legislative or executive decisions and campaign contributions. To this it may be said that since contributions are rarely given at random or to one's political enemies, the existence of this correlation is no answer to the conclusions given here. If anything, the fact that conservatives support conservative causes or candidates, or that liberals support liberal causes or candidates, suggests that the candidates and causes create the money, and not the other way round.

The testimony before the Select Committee does not affect the balance of evidence on the question. Quite the contrary, it leads to a rather different conclusion.

The Watergate break-in did not result from the Republicans' having "too much cash." While campaign money financed the break-in, the individuals involved did not happen upon the scheme while searching for ways to spend excess cash. The capability and inclination to embark on such undertakings was established independently of the campaign and its supply of money.[22] The Ellsberg psychiatrist break-in occurred well before Watergate and can in no

---

[21] V. O. Key, Jr., *Politics, Parties, and Pressure Groups*, 5th ed. (New York: T. Y. Crowell, 1964), pp. 495, 513.

[22] See, for example, testimony of E. Howard Hunt, *Select Committee Hearings*, vol. 38 (mimeo.), pp. 7584-7588. Hunt there describes the formation of the "special investigations unit" in the White House. Hunt later testified about the creation of the so-called "Gemstone" project (ibid., p. 7618), involving authorization from then Attorney General Mitchell, and that he believed information which precipitated the Watergate break-in had come from the FBI (see ibid., pp. 7694-7733).

way be traced to campaign giving. The persons employed in that burglary were largely the same as those involved in the Watergate operation and were part of the "Plumbers group" formed because of the Pentagon Papers incident and similar "leaks." One of the leaders, G. Gordon Liddy, was general counsel of the Finance Committee of the Committee to Re-Elect the President (CREP).[23]

In any event, the "too much cash" rationale has legislative implications only if the break-in was paradigmatic, rather than aberrational. The evidence demonstrates it was not a good model. Consider the following exchange between Senator Baker and Mr. Anthony Ulasewicz:

> MR. ULASEWICZ: I will tell you, any old retired man in the New York City Police Department who would become involved in a thing like that, he thought he had to for whatever reason it was, he would not have walked in with an army, that is for sure.
> SENATOR BAKER: He would not have walked in with an army. Would he have walked in with identification papers and serial numbered $100 bills and address book?
> MR. ULASEWICZ: He probably would have walked in like any decent common looking citizen, laid something in the right place and walked right out and that would have been the end of it for a long time.[24]

What the evidence shows is that the Watergate break-in was poorly planned and poorly executed. Far too many people were involved and the participants were astonishingly negligent in leaving a trail of evidence leading to CREP and the White House. Large amounts of money are unnecessary for such activities and campaign money is too easily traceable to be used in clandestine activities. Covert operations, in short, should be run only with covert money.

The outlawing of private campaign contributions and limiting of expenditures is thus an anomalous remedy, since Watergate demonstrated that campaign money is not well suited to financing illegal activities.

This solution is anomalous for yet another reason. All else being equal, the temptation to resort to illegal, covert activities such as bugging, burglary or dirty tricks in political campaigns will decrease as the soliciting and spending of campaign money is permitted and

---

[23] For a general description of the internal structure of the Committee to Re-Elect the President, see testimony of Robert C. Odle, Jr., *Select Committee Hearings*, Phase I, Book 1, pp. 9-35, *passim*.

[24] Ibid., p. 292.

increase as it is circumscribed. *To the degree that activities such as television advertising are foreclosed, the pay-off for illegal activities will seem greater to those disposed to break the law.*

It has also been asserted that the Watergate hearings "demonstrate beyond any doubt the insidious influence of private money. . . ."[25] This demonstration presumably is found in the disclosure that several corporations made contributions in violation of the Corrupt Practices Act—and, of course, also in the ITT affair and that of the milk producers.

The corporate contributions in question were, in the words of the senator quoted above, "blatant violations of the existing Federal election laws,"[26] and the outlawing of contributions now lawful seems a peculiar way of reducing contributions now unlawful—unless it is believed that federal subsidies will eliminate the temptation to solicit corporate contributions.

This expectation seems unrealistic. There is no one sum which is "adequate" for a campaign, particularly when set by legislation applying uniformly to diverse elections. There is, in addition, no reason to anticipate that Congress will fix subsidies at a high rather than a low level. The "pressure group" with the most muscle will be incumbent congressmen who, if other sources of funds are outlawed, are likely to prefer modest subsidies, which will disadvantage challengers while mollifying taxpayers.

The expectation is unrealistic for yet another reason. If corporate executives take the risk of illegal corporate contributions when unlimited individual gifts are permissible, the outlawing of individual gifts would, if anything, increase the temptation to resort to corporate donations, for they would be no more risky legally, but considerably less expensive personally, than the alternative.[27]

Calls for the outlawing of private financing mistake the lessons of the corporate misdeeds and of the Vice-President's resignation. Virtually all the corporations gave, not in expectation of some specific reward, but out of fear of retaliation by the government. This fear is engendered by the existing scheme of economic regulation which endows the executive branch with unchecked power to give and take

---

[25] See note 6, Introduction, *supra.*

[26] Ibid.

[27] Experience with subsidies in Puerto Rico, to use a comparable example, demonstrates that the subsidies are used up before the election, and that the illegal solicitation of funds from government employees ensues. Henry Wells and Robert Anderson, *Government Financing of Political Parties in Puerto Rico: A Supplement to Study Number Four* (Princeton, N. J.: Citizens' Research Foundation, 1966), p. 5.

away economic benefits.[28] The power and the fear will survive the outlawing of private campaign contributions. Indeed, the lesson of the Vice-President's resignation seems clearly to be that money flows toward the locus of discretionary power but not necessarily in the form of campaign contributions. Had the state of Maryland enjoyed during Mr. Agnew's governorship every reform now proposed, Gerald Ford would still have ascended to the vice-presidency.

More support for that conviction might be found in the ITT and milk producers' affairs. At best, however, the evidence shows no more than isolated instances of abuse not inconsistent with the conclusions of existing scholarship. While there is evidence of improper motive on ITT's part, the antitrust settlement is regarded by credible observers such as Archibald Cox as a "perfectly good bargain" so far as the government is concerned.[29] In the case of the milk producers, the form of economic regulation involved is uniquely susceptible to abuse. There is no reason why milk prices should be set by the President and even if every allegation made about the affair is true, the elimination of private campaign financing will not eliminate the system which generates the abuse.

The case against private campaign financing is not, on the available evidence, powerful. Sensationalized and impressionistic, it rests more on horror stories than on sustained scholarship. Still, abuses do exist; some functions of private money are undesirable; and the case against private financing might well be adequate in the absence of a case for it. An affirmative case can be made, however.

Private Campaign Financing: Its Positive Functions. That private financing influences the political process cannot be doubted; but it also cannot be doubted that it is only one of many factors having such an impact. Still, why should it have any influence at all? A political system in which elections are determined on a "one man, one vote" basis, it might be argued, ought not permit an unequally distributed resource to affect the political process.

This is a simplistic view of that process, a view which misconceives the nature of the consent of the governed and the need for

---

[28] See, for example, testimony of George A. Spater, *Select Committee Hearings,* reported in Mark R. Arnold, "Paying for Politics," *The National Observer,* December 8, 1973, p. 2, col. 4.

[29] Testimony of Archibald Cox, *Hearings on the Special Prosecutor before the Committee on the Judiciary, United States Senate,* 93rd Congress, 1st session (1973), p. 52.

individual political freedom in a democratic society. As Alexander M. Bickel has said:

> What is above all important is consent—not a presumed theoretical consent, but a continuous actual one, born of continual responsiveness. There is popular sovereignty, and there are votes in which majorities or pluralities prevail, but that is not nearly all. Majorities are in large part fictions. They exist only on election day and they can be registered on a very few issues. To be responsive and to enjoy consent, government must register numerous expressions of need and interest by numerous groups, and it must register relative intensities of need and interest.[30]

It is in order to "register numerous expressions of need and interest" that all kinds of activities, in addition to periodic elections, may legitimately affect political outcomes. Demonstrations, public hearings, handbills, lobbying, study groups, letters to congressmen, books, articles, organizational activities, petitions, advertisements, rallies and acts of civil disobedience all influence the political process in a way that is inconsistent with simplistic notions of "one man, one vote." However nice a ring the slogan has, it cannot be the exclusive basis of a political system without restricting individual freedom and creating instability by excluding legitimate and intensely held political claims. "One man, one vote" may be a convenient basis for *apportioning* legislative districts.[31] As a full political system it is not consistent with larger notions of freedom and of the consent of the governed.

Private campaign financing can thus be viewed as an aspect of political freedom. All political activities make claims on society's resources. Speeches, advertisements, broadcasts, canvassing, volunteer work—all consume resources. Money is the medium of exchange by which individuals employ resources owned by others. If political activities are left to private financing, individuals are free to choose which activities to engage in, on behalf of which causes, or whether to do so at all. When the individual is deprived of this choice, either because government limits or prohibits his using money for political purposes or takes his money in taxes and subsidizes the political activities it chooses, his freedom is impaired.

---

[30] Alexander M. Bickel, "Watergate and the Legal Order," *Commentary*, January 1974, p. 21.

[31] Even this point is disputed. See Robert Dixon, *Democratic Representation* (New York: Oxford University Press, 1968).

Money is fungible with other resources suitable for political use and, distributional questions apart, the individual who contributes a resource directly, for example, time and labor, is in many ways indistinguishable from the individual who contributes money which in turn purchases time and labor. Money, it must be conceded though, is the most "fungible" resource.

Campaign contributions, therefore, perform honorable and important functions. The contribution of money allows citizens to participate in the political process. Persons without much free time have few alternatives to monetary contributions other than inaction.

Campaign contributions are also vehicles of expression for donors seeking to persuade other citizens on public issues. Contributing to a candidate permits individuals to pool resources and voice their message far more effectively than if each spoke singly. This is critically important because it permits citizens to join a potent organization and propagate their views *beyond their voting districts*. Persons who feel strongly about appointments to the Supreme Court, for example, can demonstrate their convictions by contributing to the campaigns of sympathetic senators.

Nor is there anything inherently wrong with contributing to candidates who agree with one's views on social and economic policies, even where those policies may benefit the donor. Obviously, groups pursue their self-interests and seek support from others. *That is a salient characteristic of a free political system.* Those who seek to regulate that kind of contribution can stand with those who would deny the vote to welfare recipients to prevent that vote from being "bought" by promises of higher benefits. So long as we accept the bestowal of economic favor as a proper function of government, potential recipients will tend to exchange this support for such favors.

Contributions of this sort may represent broad interests that might otherwise be underrepresented. Suppose land developers mount a campaign against proposals to restrict the use of large undeveloped areas. Certainly they represent their own economic interests, but they also functionally represent potential purchasers, an "interested" group that would otherwise go unnoticed since few persons would consider themselves future purchasers at the critical moment.

These functions of campaign contributions are often ignored because critics of the present system mistake cause and effect. A senator may support union causes because he receives large union contributions but in fact it may be more likely that he receives contributions because he supports the causes.

Contributions also serve as a barometer of the intensity of voter feeling. In a majoritarian system, voters who feel exceptionally strongly about particular issues may be unable to reflect their feelings adequately in periodic votes.[32] As members of the antiwar movement often pointed out, the strength of their feelings as well as their numbers should have been taken into account. If a substantial group feels intensely about an issue, a system which does not allow that feeling to be heard effectively may well be endangered. Campaign contributions are perhaps the most important, and least offensive, means by which the intensity of feeling can be expressed. People who feel strongly about United States support for Israel, for example, are able to voice that conviction with greater effect through carefully directed campaign donations than in periodic elections in which the stance of the available candidates does not permit a clear signal to be given.

This function might be discounted if large contributions reflected only intense but idiosyncratic views. For the most part, however, intense feelings will not generate substantial funds unless large numbers of citizens without great wealth also share those convictions. Campaign contributors in these circumstances serve as representatives or surrogates for the entire group. That Mr. X, who favors free trade, can make larger contributions than Mr. Y, who does not, really matters little, if Mr. Z agrees with Mr. Y and gives heavily.

Candidates seeking change, moreover, may have far greater need for, and make better use of, campaign money than those with established images or those defending the existing system. Money is, after all, subject to the law of diminishing returns and thus generally of less use to the well-known politician than to the newcomer. The existence of "seed money" may be an important agent of change.[33]

The challenge to the arguments that private campaign financing enlarges political freedom and contributes stability to the system is essentially distributional: because money is maldistributed throughout the society, its use in political campaigns undesirably skews the political process by allowing wealthy individuals too much power. As noted in the previous section, present evidence does not demonstrate that monetary support is available only for certain ideas. Quite the contrary, it strongly suggests that a wide array of causes and

---

[32] See generally, Robert A. Dahl, *A Preface to Democratic Theory* (Chicago: University of Chicago Press, 1956).

[33] See Lester G. Telser, "Advertising and Competition," *Journal of Political Economy*, December 1964, p. 537, which finds that advertising is most effective in introducing new products.

movements on the right and left can attract money. Still, individuals can increase their *personal* political power through contributions, and even if they functionally represent like-thinking but poorer people, it might be argued that wealth nevertheless is skewing the process.

This argument rests on the assumption that by reducing the personal political power of the large contributor, political influence will be spread more evenly through the society. Such an assumption seems almost surely wrong, for limitations on the use of money may aggravate rather than diminish any distortion. Direct access to the resources most useful for political purposes may be even more unevenly distributed than wealth.

For example, restrictions on private campaign financing may well enhance the power of those who control the media, particularly if public subsidies are modest in size and thus increase candidate dependence on the goodwill of the media. Limitations on the use of money must also increase the relative power of individuals with large amounts of free time and the ability to attract public attention. Finally, groups with the ability to take their money "underground" and operate independent "issue" (rather than "political") campaigns will have their power increased. It has been reported, for example, that unions favor a ban on contributions because their own power would be relatively increased as a result of the host of "indirect contributions" they can provide.[34]

What emerges is the likelihood that restrictions on private campaign financing will not increase the political power of the people generally but will further concentrate it in already powerful segments of the community. Ironically, the increment will largely fall to various sectors of the well-to-do, because direct access to resources useful for political purposes (free time, control of the media, ability to operate "issue" campaigns) is concentrated not in the poor but in the wealthy. Private campaign financing in short may in fact be a means of spreading political power and expanding the range of discourse.

The call for regulation of campaign financing can be extended to other kinds of resources and could easily become a call for substantial limitations on political freedom. The allegations about the influence of money reflect a basic and disturbing mistrust of the people. If campaign financing really "distorts" legislative or executive behavior, candidates can raise its effect as an issue and the voters can respond at election time. The call for legislation must be based on the

---

[34] Byron E. Calame, "Unions and Politics," *The Wall Street Journal*, January 29, 1974, pp. 1, 29.

belief that the voters cannot be relied upon to perceive their own best interests. If one really believes the people are this easily fooled and in need of this protection, however, there may be no end to the campaign tactics eligible for regulation and no end to calls for increases in the power of those "protecting" the public.

Campaign Financing and the Law. A number of general considerations applying to the regulation of campaign financing deserve independent discussion. First, regulation must be enacted by incumbents who are not likely to pass legislation that will reduce their power. How those who allege that campaign money has such a corrupting effect on legislators can expect them to enact "neutral" regulations on its use is one of the great mysteries of the present debate.

The influence of self-interest on legislation regulating political financing is everywhere to be seen by those who care to look. The first effective legislation was a limit on campaign expenditures, an act generally favoring incumbents who have an established image. Everyone agrees, moreover, that congressmen receive an advantage from governmental subsidies such as offices, the frank, paid staffs, and so on. These are subject to the control of incumbents and are frequently augmented. Removing these advantages (or, in the alternative, giving challengers an offsetting subsidy) can be justified, but the record indicates that such legislation is politically unlikely. That fact alone casts the shadow of suspicion over any measure that can pass.

Free societies should shun all regulation of political speech—including regulation which claims to eliminate "distortions" or to protect the public from being fooled. No one has a monopoly on political truth, and the claim that laws are needed to "correct"[35] the electoral process by regulating campaign advocacy should be viewed with alarm, particularly when the laws are passed by interested parties. Mr. Justice Holmes once said, in a justly famous passage:

> But when men have realized that time has upset many fighting faiths they may come to believe even more than they believe the very foundations of their own conduct that the ultimate good desired is better reached by free trade in ideas—that the best test of truth is the power of the thought to get itself accepted in the competition of the market. . . .[36]

Those who urge extensive regulation of campaign financing do not share Justice Holmes's faith in the free marketplace of ideas.

---

[35] See statement of Russell D. Hemenway, national director, National Committee for an Effective Congress, in *Hearings on S. 372*, p. 165.

[36] Abrams v. United States, 250 U.S. 616, 630 (Holmes, J., dissenting).

Because all such legislation intrudes on freedom of expression, constitutional precedent requires that it be carefully and narrowly tailored to the harm it seeks to cure. Thus where "less drastic" measures are available to achieve the congressional objective, the courts will invalidate a statute which encroaches on individual liberties.[37] Many of the proposals now under consideration seem overly broad, for they lump all contributions together, making no distinctions as to their sources or kinds.[38]

Even with full credit given to all the allegations, the call for overarching restrictive laws cannot be justified. Ambassadorial appointments, for instance, are subject to a veto by the same Senate that seeks to regulate campaign financing. Similarly, if government contracts are being awarded to large campaign contributors, the irresistible conclusion is that the process of determining awards is fundamentally wrong. Ending the use of private money will not eliminate political influence. Contracts will simply be awarded to those displaying political loyalty in other ways. Those who would regulate political financing should also look to reducing superfluous economic regulation. If milk producers make contributions in return for higher price supports, why should not this subsidy and all discretionary subsidy programs be repealed? It is no answer to say that well-placed contributions make repeal politically impossible, since that argument applies with even more convincing force to legislation forbidding contributions. Finally, if campaign money is turned to illegal purposes, the law may require that no contributions larger than $25 be in cash so that "laundering" would be rendered even more difficult.

The furor over private campaign financing is likely to obscure one of the few clear lessons of Watergate, the lesson that the unchecked discretion to bestow or take away economic favors permits

---

[37] In Aptheker v. Secretary of State, 378 U.S. 500 (1964), the Supreme Court declared unconstitutional Section 6 of the Subversive Activities Control Act of 1950, 50 U.S.C., Section 785. That statute denied to any member of a registered Communist organization (or one ordered to be registered) the right to apply for a passport, or for the renewal of a passport, or to attempt to use any such passport, knowing of the registration. The Court, in an opinion by Justice Goldberg, noted that "in determining the constitutionality of Section 6, it is also important to consider that Congress has within its power 'less drastic' means of achieving the congressional objective of safeguarding our national security. . . . The section judged by its plain import and by the substantive evil which Congress sought to control, sweeps too widely and too indiscriminately across the liberty guaranteed by the First Amendment. . . . here, as elsewhere, precision must be the touchstone of legislation so affecting basic freedoms." 378 U.S. 500, pp. 512-514.

[38] For example, all contributions over $100 must, even under present law, be disclosed (2 U.S.C., Sections 431-434).

governmental officials to wield arbitrary power. Only the imposition of controls on the exercise of that power can solve the underlying evil. Attacks on private campaign contributions are a cure aimed at a symptom rather than a cause.

Nothing demonstrates this so much as Vice-President Agnew's resignation. Both Mr. Agnew[39] and critics of private campaign contributions[40] have for their own purposes suggested that a need for public financing was somehow demonstrated by the plight in which he found himself. Yet he admittedly did not use the money received for political purposes, and the donors knew it. What the Agnew affair proves beyond question, therefore, is that even if there were a system of public financing, the money would have changed hands.

In addition, regulating campaign financing through the criminal law necessarily contemplates trials of political figures after elections. The danger in this, one hopes, is evident to all, for prosecutions are all too subject to political influence and all too effective a means of silencing one's opponents. Such a "reform" hardly seems tailored to the abuses uncovered by the Watergate investigation. The danger is not the less because present law contains so many complex requirements and contemplates such extensive bookkeeping that violations are all but unavoidable.

Furthermore, all regulation of campaign financing is based on a distinction between election campaigns and political and propaganda activities which occur between elections. But, if money is all that powerful a deceiver, it will work its evil ways between campaigns as well as during them. Indeed, since major shifts in public opinion generally occur during that period rather than during campaigns,[41] it may well be most effective then.

The law compels business and union groups, for example, to make an irrational distinction between "political" activities (during the campaign) and "educational" activities (during the interim). The only functional distinction between the periods is that the activities in the former tend to focus on particular candidates. Candidates are often known well in advance and activities designed to influence their election go on for months before the formal campaign. Laws regulating campaign financing thus compel accounting distinctions without political significance.

1. *Limitations on Expenditures and Contributions: Price Controls in the Marketplace of Ideas.* These limitations fall into two categories.

---

[39] See TV address of Spiro T. Agnew, *New York Times*, October 16, 1973, p. 34.
[40] See note 6, Introduction, *supra*.
[41] See note 4, Chapter 1, *supra*.

(a) The first is limits on spending by candidates. Those who seek to impose limits on expenditures by candidates face a dilemma of constitutional dimensions. On the one hand, if the limitation applies only to expenditures explicitly authorized by the candidate, it will be, in Lyndon Johnson's famous phrase, "more loophole than law." "Independent" committees will carry on the campaign. On the other hand, if it seeks to charge the candidate with all outlays from whatever source that further his candidacy, it must give the candidate a veto over all those who would support him through monetary expenditures. The campaign spending law of 1971 thus prohibits the media from charging for political advertising unless the candidate certifies that the charge will not cause his spending to exceed the limit.[42] The effect, therefore, is to restrict the freedom of individuals to buy political advertising supporting or, in some circumstances (under the regulations promulgated by the comptroller general of the United States),[43] attacking a candidate.

This statute has been greeted by constitutional authorities with comments varying from "would seem to violate the First Amendment"[44] to "flatly unconstitutional."[45] It has, moreover, been held an unconstitutional prior restraint on the media by a three-judge dis-

---

[42] 47 U.S.C., Section 803(b) states that "No person may make any charge for the use by or on behalf of any legally qualified candidate for Federal elective office (or for nomination to such office) of any newspaper, magazine, or outdoor advertising facility, unless such candidate (or a person specifically authorized by such candidate in writing to do so) certifies in writing to the person making such charge that the payment of such charge will not violate paragraph (1), (2), or (3) of subsection (a) of this section, whichever is applicable."

[43] 11 C.F.R., Section 4.5, "Amounts spent urging candidate's defeat or derogating his stand," states that "(a) An expenditure for the use of communications media opposing or urging the defeat of a Federal candidate, or derogating his stand on campaign issues, shall not be deemed to be an expenditure for the use of communications media on behalf of any other Federal candidate and shall not be charged against any other Federal candidate's applicable expenditure limitation under section 104(a) of the Act and this part, unless such other Federal candidate has directly or indirectly authorized such use or unless the circumstances of such use taken as a whole are such that consent may reasonably be imputed to such other candidate." What may or may not be "reasonably imputed to such other candidate" is not described with any specificity.

[44] A. Rosenthal, *Federal Regulation of Campaign Finance: Some Constitutional Questions* (Princeton, N. J.: Citizens' Research Foundation, 1972), p. 63.

[45] Statement of Alexander Bickel, ibid., p. 66. See also, for discussions of this point, Martin H. Redish, "Campaign Spending Laws and the First Amendment," *N.Y.U. Law Review*, vol. 46 (1971), p. 900, and Joel L. Fleishman, "Freedom of Speech and Equality of Political Opportunity: The Constitutionality of the Federal Election Campaign Act of 1971," *North Carolina Law Review*, vol. 51, p. 389. And see, Thomas I. Emerson, *The System of Freedom of Expression* (New York: Random House, 1970), p. 639.

trict court of the District of Columbia (Judges Bazelon, Bryant and Parker).[46]

In light of Supreme Court decisions, the likelihood that such laws are beyond Congress's power is quite high. In *New York Times* v. *Sullivan*, the Court held that a newspaper advertisement on public issues was entitled to First Amendment protection.[47] The fact that the advertisement was purchased was "immaterial."[48] In *Eastern Railroad President's Conference* v. *Noerr Motor Freight*, moreover, the Court held that the Sherman Act did not apply to advertisements intended to influence legislation specifically designed to injure competitors.[49] In that case, certain railroad companies had conducted a publicity campaign which was "vicious, corrupt, and fraudulent" and "designed to foster the adoption and retention of laws and law enforcement practices destructive of the trucking business. . . ."[50] Rejecting the claim that such activities violated the Sherman Act, the Supreme Court, through Mr. Justice Black, stated,

> It is neither unusual nor illegal for people to seek action on laws in the hope that they may bring about an advantage to themselves and a disadvantage to their competitors. . . . To disqualify people from taking a public position in matters in which they are financially interested would thus deprive the government of a valuable source of information and . . . deprive the people of their right to petition in the very instances in which that right may be of the most importance to them.[51]

The entire theory of the decision rests on the First Amendment policy of protecting groups in their efforts to influence government to act in their interests. The efforts in this case—the financing of a systematic publicity campaign designed to induce favorable governmental action—are of particular relevance to this discussion. If Congress cannot stop individuals from conducting the kind of campaigns that were involved in *Noerr*, surely it cannot do so when the issue is the election of an individual to office.

The First Amendment has given rise to considerable disagreement over its scope. All agree, however, that it protects political

---

[46] American Civil Liberties Union v. Jennings, Civil No. 1967-72 (D.D.C., opinion filed on November 14, 1973), mimeo. opinion.

[47] 376 U.S. 254 (1964).

[48] Ibid., p. 266.

[49] 365 U.S. 126 (1961).

[50] Ibid., p. 129.

[51] Ibid., p. 127.

speech. If we are to have "free trade in ideas" in the political sphere, individual citizens must be able to express whatever ideas they choose in whatever form they believe appropriate, whether or not it costs them money. There is no room for price controls in the marketplace of ideas.

Setting a limit on candidate expenditures sets a maximum on the political activities in which American citizens can engage. It is thus unconstitutional. The reasoning that speech which costs money is too persuasive [52] cannot be limited to campaign financing. For one can also argue that demonstrations of more than a certain number of people, extensive voter canvassing, or too many billboards with catchy slogans also "distort" public opinion and ought to be regulated.

The freedom to speak is not the only liberty infringed by such legislation. Because giving to a candidate permits individuals to "pool" their contributions and act as part of an effective organization, limitations on candidate spending are in effect restrictions on the freedom of association.

(b) The second category of limitations is limits on individual contributions. Except where someone seeks personal gain in direct exchange for a campaign contribution, individual donations are political activities. Limitations on their size are thus an explicit restriction on political freedom. If a person feels strongly about the defense of Israel, the conduct of the Indochina War, or the continuation of farm subsidies, he should have the right to finance appropriate political activities, whether or not those activities are part of a political campaign.

Government regulation establishes a dangerous precedent. If one can limit the size of individual contributions, why cannot (or should not) the government limit the extent of voluntary activity on behalf of candidates? Both involve giving a thing of value to a candidate, and both are designed to further his candidacy. Both, moreover, create obligations. The only distinction is between the use of time and effort directly for the candidate and the use of income gained through the expenditure of time and effort. These activities are largely fungible, a fact that Congress recognized when it specifically excepted volunteer services from the definition of "contribution" in the 1971 statute. [53]

---

[52] See press release of Senator Edmund S. Muskie, "Muskie Urges Media Campaign Reforms, Scores Nixon's Attitude," March 3, 1971, p. 2: "Ideally, a limit on all spending would be best. But a limit on media spending would be an effective control over spending because television and radio have such a unique role in public persuasiveness."

[53] 18 U.S.C., Section 591(e)(5).

Although the author believes that limitations on individual contributions are unconstitutional, it should be noted that the case against these is not as strong as is the case against limitations on candidate expenditures which entail a veto on political advertising by individuals. In the latter case a complete ban is involved, while in the former it is a matter of degree. Under this view, the constitutional issue would turn on how low the limitation was. There is a practical risk in limiting the size of individual contributions, however. If the Supreme Court were to affirm the district court decision striking down the candidate's veto over individual spending but uphold a low limit on contributions to candidates, the effect would be the opposite of what was intended. The wealthy would be able to conduct their independent advertising campaigns while all others would be limited in their ability to pool resources behind a candidate. Congress should not, therefore, limit the size of individual contributions until this constitutional issue has been resolved by the Supreme Court.

2. *Reporting and Disclosure Legislation.* Laws calling for disclosure of campaign contributions require that political acts of individuals be registered with the government and publicized. They are designed to inform the public of the size and source of a candidate's campaign funds so that the voter may better estimate the independence of his future conduct and, perhaps, see how others perceive him. The laws may also "chill" potential contributors who fear that publicity might permit persons with different political views or affiliations— for example, clients, employers, officials who award government contracts—to retaliate against them. The evidence before the Select Committee indicated that the celebrated "enemies list" was drawn in part from lists of contributors to Democratic candidates.[54] The effect of such legislation, therefore, may be to deter political activity, a result with strong First Amendment implications.

This constitutional issue falls within a growing class of cases in which persons or organizations claim a right to anonymity in their political activities. Newsmen thus claim a privilege not to disclose sources, the NAACP has resisted the efforts of southern states to compel disclosure of its membership lists, and many say a state may not require that those who distribute handbills reveal the author or

---

[54] Contemporary observers of the Watergate hearings have almost uniformly ignored testimony that the "enemies list" was compiled in large part from lists of campaign contributors to opposition candidates. See testimony of John W. Dean III, *Select Committee Hearings*, Phase I, Book 4, p. 1410. (These documents [Exhibit 64, p. 1733, and Exhibit 65, p. 1734] were given to the committee during Mr. Dean's testimony on the compilation of the "enemies list.")

sponsor. Because there is no absolute right to anonymity, these claims have met with varying success in the Supreme Court.[55] The need for disclosure is weighed against the deterrent effect publicity may have on the exercise of civil liberties.

Existing law seems difficult to justify on that basis. For example, disclosure is required for every contribution of $100 or more to a presidential campaign.[56] Yet it is inconceivable that a contribution of that size could have an undesirable impact or, indeed, any impact. The law would seem to be overbroad and subject to constitutional challenge.

When disclosure laws focus on contributions from those doing business with the government or on large contributions, the constitutional claims against these laws lose their force. To the extent that these laws forbid anonymity to almost all contributors, however, the conclusion that the deterrent effect outweighs the need seems irresistible. While present law may be overbroad, Congress nevertheless has it within its power to pass a statute focusing more precisely on contributions with a genuine potential for abuse.

3. *Public Financing.* There is wide support for a range of proposals looking to governmental financing of campaigns for federal office. Subsidies, it is thought, will enable persons without great wealth to run for office[57] and will reduce the dependence of officeholders on a few well-to-do backers.[58] Public financing is, however, subject to many of the objections raised against limitations on spending or individual contributions.

Direct subsidies also raise serious problems of freedom of expression. They are a form of compulsory political activity which limits the freedom of those desiring to refrain from politics as well as those who wish to participate. When an individual is forced, in effect, to make a contribution to a political movement—whether he is indifferent to it, finds it distasteful or applauds it—it may fairly be said that a basic freedom is being infringed. The fact that the money is "laundered" by the Internal Revenue Service and becomes part of general revenue only adds a dash of deviousness to the proposal. When this forced payment is combined with limits on contributions to favored candidates, political freedom is drastically limited. The argument

---

[55] See, for example, Bates v. Little Rock, 361 U.S. 516, 524 (1960); Talley v. California, 362 U.S. 60 (1960); and U.S. v. Caldwell, 408 U.S. 665 (1972).

[56] 2 U.S.C., Sections 431-434.

[57] Hart bill, Section 2(1).

[58] Ibid., Section 2(2).

here is analogous to that used in church-state matters. Many who today propose political subsidies condemn subsidies where religious organizations are concerned. The precise constitutional issues differ but they are sufficiently analogous that one may well argue that the underlying principle is the same.

Many of the subsidy proposals are not well thought out. The Kennedy-Scott proposal, for example, virtually bars private financing in presidential elections while providing very modest governmental financing.[59] Consider the advantage this would give an incumbent President running for reelection. Able as always to make "news" or to use Air Force One on "nonpolitical" trips, he could campaign extensively while his opponent was restricted to a sum much less than that raised by presidential candidate Senator George McGovern in 1972.[60]

Even when private financing is not barred, subsidy plans are not well conceived either as to need or impact. They are a classic case of tactics obscuring the strategic issue, their proponents being more concerned with obtaining legislation somehow embodying public financing than with worrying about the "details." But attention to the "details" reveals a host of problems of principle as well as practice.

Unrestricted access to subsidies is an incentive to everyone with a yen for publicity to become a candidate. Elections might become an anarchic jungle with policy issues wholly obscured. Such a result can be avoided by giving subsidies directly to parties but to do this does nothing to increase individual opportunity and merely encourages the formation of an endless number of parties.

Subsidy proposals must, therefore, contain limitations on eligibility. One kind of formula might call for a subsidy adjusted to performance in previous elections. This seems unfair to newcomers, overly generous to the "old guard," and irrelevant to the goal of increasing opportunity. Another formula adjusts the subsidy to performance in the election itself. For example, the Hart bill (which applies only to Senate and House races but could easily be extended to presidential campaigns) would require a security deposit equal to one-fifth of the anticipated subsidy. If the candidate received less than 10 percent of the total vote, the deposit would be forfeited. If he received less than 5 percent, he would have to repay whatever subsidy he had received.[61]

---

[59] Amendment to H.R. 11104, 93rd Congress, 1st session (1973), reprinted in *Congressional Record*, November 15, 1973, p. S 20451.

[60] Ibid., and see note 9, Chapter 1, *supra*.

[61] Hart bill, Section 7(a).

This provision, however, is hardly consistent with the bill's ostensible purpose. A candidate without access to funds might well have no chance under such a law. If he refused the subsidy, it would be a signal that he did not take his chances seriously. He would then be quite unlikely to raise substantial funds, unless he had a rich patron, a result counterproductive so far as the purpose of the legislation is concerned. (This alternative would be closed off if there were limits on individual contributions.) If he took the subsidy, he would risk bankruptcy. The Hart formula is a Trojan horse to the candidate without access to a sizeable campaign war chest.

What such a formula would create, however, is a temptation for those who anticipate financial gain from running for office. Under the Hart plan, an author/candidate might be encouraged to enter the race to gather material for a book. A publisher's advance could cover the cost of posting the security bond or returning the subsidy. Similarly, many young lawyers would be likely to find it profitable to enter congressional races and take their chances on the subsidy in order to get publicity beneficial to their practice. Even if they had to forfeit their bond or return the subsidy, it might seem profitable when the subsidy was capitalized over the period of time the anticipated income would accrue. The Hart formula might thus increase the number of nonserious candidates while discouraging those the bill is designed to aid.

Direct subsidization of campaigns would have an enormous although uncertain impact on third parties. If a formula like that contained in the Hart bill were employed, third parties would have to gamble in deciding whether to take the subsidy. The "seriousness" of the party would have little to do with its decisions since, although early showings in the polls might augur well, all third parties suffer late in campaigns from the urge of voters to make their votes "count." Declining the subsidy would be taken to mean that the party was not serious and, in any event, the possibility of a subsidy would deter further giving. If the formula were based on showings in previous elections, subsidies might sustain third parties long after their appeal had diminished, simply because they once received a significant portion of the vote.

In fact, any formula for determining who gets what subsidy is likely to be viewed as unfair to someone and perhaps open to constitutional challenge. Subsidies are inherently inconsistent with a "free trade in ideas." One commentator has stated it in this way:

> The traditional meaning of this concept is that government must not interfere on behalf of either a majority or

a minority; if the majority's superior resources give it greater power to express its views through the mass media, this is a natural and proper result of the superior appeal the majority's "product" has to the public. Government intervention on behalf of minorities would deny first and fourteenth amendment rights to members of the majority group by undermining the preponderance which the free market has given them. Likewise, state action calculated to reduce the relative power of minorities to express their views would infringe their constitutional rights. A plan allocating funds to all parties equally would give minorities publicity out of proportion to the size of their following thus discriminating against the majority, and a plan apportioning funds according to party size would give the majority more funds with which to influence uncommitted voters, tending to increase the majority's preponderance.[62]

Quite apart from the dilemma of choosing a formula for eligibility,[63] subsidy proposals show other evidence of not being well thought out. The existence of subsidies might well decrease citizen participation and the morale of those active in politics. Such was the result of subsidies in Puerto Rico where, over time, party morale declined and voter interest in party activities was correspondingly reduced.[64] Subsidies, in short, might increase the distance between voters and candidates.

Public financing might also endanger the delicate balance of the American party system. If the subsidy were to go to candidates directly—as it must if the "poor" candidate is to be helped—party

---

[62] "Note, Payment of State Funds to Political Party Committees for Use in Meeting Campaign Expenses Lacks a Public Purpose," *Harvard Law Review,* vol. 78, pp. 1260, 1262-1263. See also Williams v. Rhodes, 393 U.S. 23 (1968). There an Ohio law which made it difficult for third parties to get on the ballot was considered. Justice Black, writing for the majority, noted that "there is, of course, no reason why two parties should retain a permanent monopoly on the right to have people vote for or against them. Competition in ideas and governmental policies is at the core of our electoral process and of the First Amendment freedoms" (393 U.S. 32). Similar considerations would seem to apply to a subsidy which gave third parties less than major parties.

[63] A subsidy proposed for Massachusetts in 1964 would have allocated $200,000 to the two major parties in proportion to each party's share of the total vote in the last state primary. This formula would have given the Democratic Party the great bulk of the subsidy. An Opinion of the Justices, 347 Mass. 797, 197 N.E. 2d 691 (1964), however, found the then-pending legislation not to be for a "public purpose" under state law, thus strongly implying that the bill's constitutionality was doubtful.

[64] Committee for Economic Development, *Financing a Better Election System* (New York, 1968), p. 48.

organizations would be considerably weakened. The subsidy question can be rationally answered only after a number of normative as well as empirical inquiries into the nature of the American party system have been satisfactorily resolved. Do we need stronger national parties or stronger state parties? Do we need more candidates independent of existing party organizations, or more organizations such as the Committee to Re-Elect the President? Do we need more party solidarity or will this simply lead to greater executive power?

There are no settled answers to any of these questions. Yet the proposals now before Congress may change our present system radically and rapidly. The danger is not the less because the effect is random or unintentional.

Private money is said to have weakened public confidence in the democratic process. We ought to ask, however, whether confidence is likely to be restored when taxpayers pay for campaigns they regard as frivolous, wasteful, and in some cases abhorrent. Would the taxpayer viewing television spots have more confidence in the political process because part of the cost came out of his paycheck? Would the voter have more confidence in the system because he paid for activities with which he disagreed? What if a racist ran for office and delivered radical, insulting and quasi-violent speeches? One result might be cries for even more regulation—in particular, for regulation of the content of political speech. Those calling for public financing often point to polls showing public discontent with the high cost of campaigns. The same polls, however, show as much discontent with "too much mudslinging."[65] Indeed, the question—Why should the public pay for such a thing?—seems a natural response to repugnant campaign rhetoric.

Finally, we are told that subsidies will "reduce the pressure on Congressional candidates for dependence on large campaign contributions from private sources. . . ."[66] If, however, one reduces the pressure on candidates to look to the views of contributors, to whom will the candidates look instead? It has been said, for example, that Senator McGovern's campaign speeches on Vietnam were motivated more by a desire to reach contributors than voters in general.[67] The need to raise money compels candidates to address those matters about which large groups feel strongly. Candidates might well, upon receiving campaign money from the government, mute their views. Eliminate

---

[65] The results are from a Gallup poll reprinted in *Hearings on S. 372*, p. 456.

[66] Hart bill, Section 2(4).

[67] Xandra Kayden, "The Political Campaign as an Organization," *Public Policy* (Spring 1973), vol. 21, no. 2, p. 274.

the need for money and you may eliminate much of the motive to face the issues. Attention-getting gimmicks might replace attention-getting policy statements. A subsidy combined with spending limits might thus insulate incumbents both from challengers and from the strongly held views of constituents.

Legislating a Consensual Approach. Serious problems exist, therefore, with present proposals to regulate campaign money. All entail the regulation of political speech or individual political activity and seem too easily manipulated by those in power. For Watergate to lead to "reform" perpetuating the power of those in office while limiting political freedom would be a cruel irony.

The proposals are also arbitrary in a regulatory sense. Every election is *sui generis*. The "right" amount of money necessary to an adequate campaign will differ from year to year, place to place, office to office, and candidate to candidate. Costs vary widely among geographic areas, and the usefulness of particular campaign techniques depends on a variety of changing factors. Consider, for example, the wide variations in costs and efficiency of television in congressional campaigns. The very attempt to impose general rules—so many dollars per voter, so much for television, and the like—inevitably calls for arbitrary standards.

There is an approach which avoids these dangers, and which spotlights the problem of campaign money in a way that will tend to minimize its harmful aspects. In a number of recent elections, candidates have reached agreements as to limitations on expenditures. This is suggestive. Congress should consider establishing mechanisms which encourage the formation of such contracts and provide for their enforcement.

Contracts between candidates might contain provisions on how much each can spend, how money is to be allocated among various kinds of campaign activities, what kinds of techniques may be used to raise money, and which contributions must be disclosed. Resort to a consensual approach would open up a range of possibilities limited only by the boundaries of imagination. A contract might, for example, provide that all contributions go through a central clearinghouse, a bank, for example, which could verify their legality and keep appropriate records open for all to see. A consensual approach would also avoid the arbitrariness of uniform rules applying to all elections, as well as the risk that legislation will be designed by incumbents to aid incumbents.

Candidate contracts do not rely on regulation of political speech or direct restrictions on individual liberties. Where individuals or groups seeking a candidate's election spend significant sums but are not controlled by him, the candidates can agree to exert their "best efforts" to put an end to any activities which, if "counted" in the candidate's account, would exceed the contract limit. Should such efforts fail, the contract might provide for recision or other remedies such as an upward revision of spending limits.

This does not, to be sure, solve the "loophole" problem, for a desperate candidate might well resort to the "independent" committee device to evade contract limits. Still, a consensual approach seems superior to the older law which was circumvented at will and the 1971 act which has given rise to such serious constitutional issues. Because expenditure limits must be agreed to by the candidates, they will tend to be realistic and both the need and temptation to exceed them will not frequently arise. In addition, because the sanctions would be essentially political rather than criminal, a fact-finding tribunal may not be reluctant to find actual control or failure to exert "best efforts" by a candidate.

Agreements between candidates ought to provide for arbitration of disputes over interpretation and application and Congress should provide for the enforcement of arbitration clauses in the federal courts. The arbitrator should be empowered to make findings of fact which candidates could publicize or to fashion other remedies—a prohibition on spending exceeding contract limits, for example—enforceable on review by the court.

Consensual rather than compulsory regulation also offers no guarantee that the harmful aspects of campaign money will be eliminated. Nevertheless, candidates have made such contracts in the absence of legislation, and the very existence of an enforcement mechanism will create considerable political pressure to reach agreements of this sort. Candidates will be better able to raise the issue visibly and forcefully and, if their opponents do not agree to a reasonable offer, the public can show its feelings through its vote. This proposal thus relies heavily upon democratic methods for its sanctions. If the public cares, the pressure to reach an agreement will be considerable. If it does not, the pressure will be minimal. But if the public is truly indifferent, any form of government regulation would be undesirable because it must be imposed from above by incumbents.

A consensual approval is no panacea. It may tend to embroil elections in complex litigation which will distract both voter and candidate. This, however, is preferable to the political criminal trials which might result from the legislation now under consideration.

Regulating Campaign Tactics: The Dirty Tricks Problem

One focus of the Select Committee was on political sabotage and espionage during the 1972 campaign. The charge that someone has engaged in unethical campaign tactics is hardly novel in American politics.[68] Many have asserted, however, that the hearings uncovered unethical acts more serious than those found in the typical election. The hearings, restricted as they were to the 1972 campaign, could not verify this contention. Additionally, it was alleged, though not proven, that Republican "dirty tricks" actually affected the outcome of the Democratic party's nominating process.[69]

---

[68] See testimony of Patrick J. Buchanan, *Select Committee Hearings*, vol. 40 (mimeo.), p. 8034:

"MR. DASH: I am just asking you in the memorandum where you have indicated the nature of the danger that you saw to the country and the importance that the forces of the Republican Party including the White House be aimed at knocking out the front-runner, Mr. Muskie, how far would you go to do that. What tactics would you be willing to use?

"MR. BUCHANAN: What tactics would I be willing to use? Anything that was not immoral, unethical, illegal or unprecedented in previous Democratic campaigns."

[69] See, for example, testimony of Frank Mankiewicz, *Select Committee Hearings*, vol. 45 (mimeo.), p. 8978:

"As to the effect on the 1972 campaign of the so-called 'dirty tricks' they would appear to have been successful. The purpose of it all—the slimy letters, the forged press releases, the fake leaflets—seems to have been not to influence the result of any single primary election, but to create within the Democratic Party such a strong sense of resentment among the candidates and their followers as to make unity of the party impossible once a nominee was selected. At that, the effort seems to have been most successful.

"Workers in Senator Muskie's campaign have told me that they believed the 'dirty tricks' played on Senator Muskie in New Hampshire to have been the work of the McGovern campaign. Certainly there must have been those Humphrey and Jackson partisans who, seeing the filthy letter about their candidates in Florida, forged so as to appear to be from the Muskie campaign, must have turned their anger on the Senator from Maine."

And ibid., p. 9026:

"MR. THOMPSON: I think we have to draw an overall picture as to whether or not the falling out among the various candidates, if that is what it was, had to do with what Donald Segretti and some of his people did totally or whether it was in part due to the natural operations of a political campaign. And stories, whether they are true or not, they are designed to increase a candidate's displeasure with another candidate.

"MR. MANKIEWICZ: It is unquestionably a mixed question. There are all kinds of reasons that go into it, but I think the anger and the rancor and the bitterness was far stronger this year than it has ever been and I think it is at least in large part attributable to this kind of campaign."

For a contrary view, see ibid., vol. 42 (mimeo.), p. 8414, statement by Senator Gurney:

"SENATOR GURNEY: I might comment on that. I think everyone of the

Among the activities complained of during the 1972 campaign were: [70]

(a) opposition infiltration of a candidate's organization for the purpose of removing or photocopying of documents or other espionage; [71]

(Footnote 69 continued)

100 Senators who serve in the United States has had all kinds of dirty tricks played on him in the course of political campaigns and we expect it. I am not so sure how much it upsets us. I could give you examples in my own campaign that are far more horrendous than some of these here that worked against me that you don't really pay much attention to it because you expect some of these things.

". . . incidentally, I am not minimizing this dirty trick business. I loath it, but it is a part of politics, and it is a part of both sides of politics, all of us in politics know and expect some of these things by some of the fringe elements."

[70] This section will not consider a certain number of alleged crimes not directly involved with the campaign itself—perjury, subornation of perjury, bribery of a federal judge, bribery of a witness, lying to the FBI, contempt of court, contempt of Congress, destruction of evidence, blackmail, showing classified documents to unauthorized persons, falsifying government documents, income tax violations, embezzlement, extortion, arson, intercepting mail, and flight to avoid prosecution or testifying. For a description of these and other incidents of alleged unlawful activity, see John Hanrahan, "Watergate Opened Pandora-Like Box of Myriad Crimes," *The Washington Post*, November 22, 1973, p. M1.

[71] See testimony of John R. Buckley, *Select Committee Hearings*, vol. 43 (mimeo.), describing the activities of one Elmer Wyatt, pp. 8545-8547:

"MR. EDMISTEN: All right, now, shortly after he began working with the Muskie organization, what was he doing? What job did he get?

"MR. BUCKLEY: He did a number of things, from what he told me. He took clothes to the cleaners and he took packages to the stationery store and things of that nature. But one assignment that was to become more or less regularly his was to carry messages from the Muskie campaign headquarters to the Senator's office on Capitol Hill.

"MR. EDMISTEN: So he would gather up, you say messages—I suppose that includes documents, letters, press releases, things of that nature—and place them in some container and carry them from Muskie's headquarters here to the Senate?

"MR. BUCKLEY: That is generally accurate.

"MR. EDMISTEN: All right. Did you make an arrangement with him that he would call you after receiving the Muskie documents down there and let you look at them?

"MR. BUCKLEY: This, of course, took several weeks, probably two or three weeks, to begin this. An arrangement was made whereby he would call me when he was leaving the campaign headquarters and tell me that he was en route with a box of memoranda. Now, this would require several things. It would require, number one, that he went in that day. It would require that there was not someone accompanying him, as frequently happened; that it not be raining, because the papers then would be wet; and that I be available. I frequently was not available when he called, and other times, would be involved in agency business and could not meet him.

"MR. EDMISTEN: All right. So Mr. Wyatt would call you when you were available. Would he tell you to meet him somewhere?

"MR. BUCKLEY: Meet him on the corner, on a nearby corner.

(b) use of "smear" ads and commercials in the media with fictitious sponsorship; [72]

(*Footnote 71 continued*)

"MR. EDMISTEN: What would you do?

"MR. BUCKLEY: I would proceed to meet him at 19th and L or 20th and M.

"MR. EDMISTEN: And then you proceeded to do what?

"MR. BUCKLEY: Then we would drive for a couple of blocks and I proceeded to look at the memoranda that was in the box. . . ."

And ibid., pp. 8552-8553:

"MR. EDMISTEN: All right.

"After you would receive the box of material and you would go through it and determine what was relevant to your purposes, how did you use that machine?

"MR. BUCKLEY: There would be times when there was nothing relevant in the box and we wouldn't take any pictures.

"This is a camera, of course, this is a copy stand. These lights light up the base of it. A document in this fashion would be photographed thus (indicating).

"MR. EDMISTEN: All right.

"After taking the film, would you develop it yourself?

"MR. BUCKLEY: Yes, I would.

"MR. EDMISTEN: Where?

"MR. BUCKLEY: I would develop it at home.

"MR. EDMISTEN: Now, once the film was developed, what did you do with it?

"MR. BUCKLEY: Once the film was developed, I would deliver it to Ken Rietz and subsequently to another individual."

See also testimony of Michael M. McMinoway, ibid., vol. 44 (mimeo.), pp. 8649-8650:

"MR. DASH: Did you get for each assignment a specific instruction or were the instructions covered by the initial meeting with Mr. Stone?

"MR. McMINOWAY: The itinerary of the different assignments was set by Mr. Rainer. In other words, he would tell me to which state to travel, usually to which city, he would tell me what organization they would like to have information about, but the actual operational procedures were left entirely up to me.

"MR. DASH: Did you on a fairly regular basis send Mr. Rainer or Stone materials that you were able to get from the particular headquarters you had infiltrated?

"MR. McMINOWAY: Initially, sir, the procedure was I was supplied with a post office box in Washington, D. C., to which I would send any relative document or information that I would feel necessary to fulfill by obligation of intelligence gathering.

"MR. DASH: And you obtained these documents or any materials that you felt necessary in your assignment from inside the headquarters you had infiltrated?

"MR. McMINOWAY: The documents I referred to are not private or secret documents. These documents are documents that were planned for public inspection. I at no time during the course of my employment copied or borrowed or stole or removed any documents from the headquarters other than those which were given to me by a person in authority to pass out this information."

[72] See testimony of Donald H. Segretti, *Select Committee Hearings*, vol. 41 (mimeo.), pp. 8187-8188:

"Mr. Douglas Kelly assisted me in posting the aforementioned Muskie posters, and in placing an ad in a college newspaper stating:

(c) attempted organization by the opposition of demonstrations against candidates to prevent speeches, rallies, and other campaign activities with the identity and sponsorship of the demonstrators falsified;[73]

(d) burglary of a candidate's campaign headquarters to obtain documents, or to plant "stink bombs" or electronic surveillance equipment;[74]

(*Footnote 72 continued*)

" 'Wanted. Sincere gentleman seeks running mate. White preferred but natural sense of rhythm no obstacle. Contact E. Muskie.'

"He also helped me place an ad in the classified section of the Miami Sunday Sun-Reporter stating:

" 'Senator Muskie, would you accept a Jewish running mate?' and another ad in the same newspaper stating:

" 'Senator Muskie. You wouldn't accept a Black or an American Indian, would you accept a Jewish running mate?'

"There was also an ad that was placed in a local Cuban newspaper and on a local radio station which stated:

" 'Muskie believes all people have a right to choose any type of government that they want. The Cuban people are no exception and the United States should not interfere. If elected Muskie will attempt to ease the tensions between the United States and Cuba. He was born in Maine and is a good American. Vote for Ed. Muskie.' "

[73] See ibid., pp. 8191-8192:

"Mr. Kelly and I also distributed a flier stating, 'Come. Protest the Fat Cats with Signs.' This was in reference to the Muskie dinner. Mr. Kelly and I constructed various signs but no one showed up to protest."

See also ibid., pp. 8205-8206:

"MR. DASH: Yes. Is this a memorandum you received from Mr. Chapin at your post office box?

"MR. SEGRETTI: This was a memorandum I received, I do not believe I received it at my post office box but at my home address.

"MR. DASH: At your home address.

"The memorandum for the record states:

" 'From now on, we want to have at least one Muskie sign in among demonstrators who are demonstrating against the President. It should be MUSKIE FOR PRESIDENT in big letters and should be held in a location so that it is clearly visible.

" 'At Muskie events or events by other Democratic hopefuls, there should be a sign or two which goads them. For example, at a Muskie rally there should be a large WHY NOT A BLACK VICE PRESIDENT or perhaps WE PREFER HUMPHREY or something else that would goad him along.

" 'At Humphrey rallies there should be Muskie signs and at Kennedy rallies, there should be Muskie or Humphrey signs and so on. These signs should be well-placed in relationship to the press area so that a picture is easy to get.'

"Did you follow that recommendation?

"MR. SEGRETTI: To some extent I did, yes."

[74] As to "stink bombs," see testimony of Martin D. Kelly, *Select Committee Hearings*, vol. 42 (mimeo.), p. 8389:

"MR. LENZNER: Now, Mr. Kelly, did you also on occasion discuss with Mr.

(e) electronic surveillance of the candidates by the opposition;[75]

(Footnote 74 continued)
Segretti the use of a stink bomb or some kind of chemical to be used at political events?

"MR. KELLY: Yes, sir. I have a friend that is a chemist and he came up with a concoction. The name is butyl percaptain.

"MR. LENZNER: Could you give the spelling?

"MR. KELLY: I think it is B-U-T-Y-L P-E-R-C-A-P-T-A-I-N. He guaranteed me that it would make rotten eggs smell like a rose, which is horrible, and was. It was very, very bad stuff. It was not physically harmful, but was very, very noxious. It was terrible to have to sit there and smell it. It would cause great discomfort for anyone being near it.

"This was used—Senator Muskie had a picnic scheduled in Miami and it was so bad, even inside of a bottle, you could smell it. We had to put wax around it and put it in a coke. The way it was used, the cap was opened, the coke was dropped, and everybody thought the food was bad. So it kind of made the picnic a bad affair.

"He took some of it and used it up in Tampa, from what I understand."

As to the far more serious episodes of burglary to obtain documents or to plant electronic surveillance equipment, see, for example, testimony of James W. McCord, Jr., *Select Committee Hearings*, Phase I, Book 1, pp. 157-158:

"MR. McCORD: Mr. Liddy had told me that Mr. Mitchell, John Mitchell, liked the 'takes' in quotes; that is, the documents that had been photographed on the first entry into the Democratic National Committee headquarters and that he wanted a second photographic operation to take place and that in addition, as long as that team was going in, that Mr. Mitchell wanted, had passed instructions to Mr. Liddy to check to see what the malfunctioning of the second device that was put in, second, besides Mr. Oliver's, and see what the problem was, because it was one of the two things—either a malfunction of the equipment or the fact that the installation of the device was in a room which was surrounded by four walls. In other words, it was shielded, and he wanted this corrected and another device installed.

"He also said Mr. Mitchell wanted a room bug as opposed to a device on a telephone installed in Mr. O'Brien's office itself in order to transmit not only telephone conversations but conversations out of the room itself, beyond whatever might be spoken on the telephone.

"SENATOR BAKER: Were the same people involved in the first break-in and the second break-in?

"MR. McCORD: Those associated with the second break-in were Mr. Hunt, Mr. Liddy, and me, and four of the seven Cubans that were on the first operation, Cuban-Americans.

"SENATOR BAKER: All right, sir, would you describe for us then the responsibilities, if there was an additional responsibility, of those involved in the second break-in?

"MR. McCORD: Mr. Liddy was in overall charge of the operation. Mr. Hunt was his assistant. Mr. Barker was the team captain of the group going in. My job was that of the electronic installation and the others of the group, the other Cuban-Americans, had functions divided into two categories: one of photographing certain documents within the committee, a couple of men had the function of generally being lookouts while we were inside."

[75] See, for example, testimony of Alfred C. Baldwin III, *Select Committee Hearings*, Phase I, Book 1, pp. 400-401:

(f) forging scurrilous letters and false information about candidates on the stationery of another candidate; [76]

(g) the fraudulent extension by the opposition of invitations to the public for dinners and lunches on behalf of a candidate; [77]

(h) phone callers posing as part of a candidate's campaign organization harassing a candidate's supporters or potential supporters; [78]

(Footnote 75 continued)

"SENATOR WEICKER: About how many calls did you monitor?

"MR. BALDWIN: Approximately 200.

"SENATOR WEICKER: Will you describe how you recorded them?

"MR. BALDWIN: Initially, the first day, it was on a yellow legal pad. Mr. McCord took the actual log and copy that I had made. Subsequently, he returned to the room, I believe it was on Labor Day Monday, with an electric typewriter. He asked me to transcribe my notes into typewriter form, making up duplicate copies, an original and an onionskin. That is what I proceeded to do.

"SENATOR WEICKER: Then, who would you transmit those logs to, Mr. McCord?

"MR. BALDWIN: Mr. McCord received both the original and onionskin, that is correct."

[76] See testimony of Donald H. Segretti, *Select Committee Hearings*, vol. 41 (mimeo.), p. 8187, where the witness described the following activity:

"4. The sending of a letter on Muskie stationery accusing Senators Jackson and Humphrey of sexual improprieties. I would like to make clear that this letter was my idea and was not suggested by any other person. I assume full responsibility for its contents. Each and every allegation in the letter was untrue and without any basis in fact. It was not my desire to have anyone believe the letter, but instead it was intended to create confusion among the various candidates. It is my belief that from 20 to 40 such letters were sent out, mainly to Senator Jackson's supporters. I deeply regret that I initiated this incident and wish to apologize publicly for this stupid act. I can only hope that this apology will in some way rectify the harm done to these Senators and their families."

[77] See testimony of Donald H. Segretti, ibid., p. 8188:

"We also distributed some fliers inviting the public to a non-existent open house at Muskie's headquarters in Miami."

And p. 8191:

"In addition, we invited certain foreign guests and provided for their delivery to the dinner by chauffered limousine."

[78] See, for example, testimony of Michael M. McMinoway, *Select Committee Hearings*, vol. 44 (mimeo.), pp. 8667-8672, for an example of how a candidate's phones were used for harassment:

"MR. McMINOWAY: Initially, the Humphrey headquarters in Philadelphia had set up a phone bank headquarters separate from the main headquarters. It was a building, two, three story building. On the second floor there were 20 phones, they had operators at these phones, that they used a system that Mayor Rizzo initiated in his successful candidacy for the Mayor of Philadelphia, whereby they would take cross index cards of streets or blocks as they referred to them and he would call all the people on the respective blocks until they found a worker that would volunteer to be a block captain and represent the

Humphrey people in that area, and the purpose of this was to have an outlet for their literature and their campaign propaganda and to help get out the vote on election day and so forth.

"MR. DASH: And you were put in charge of that phone bank operation or supervisor?

"MR. McMINOWAY: I was assigned to help supervise it. I was not put in charge but—

"MR. DASH: Now, after you had that assignment of supervisor you began to sort of mess up the program, did you not?

"MR. McMINOWAY: I did not help the situation any.

"MR. DASH: Let me just read on April 11th in your Philadelphia diary downwards the bottom you wrote 'I promptly put people on calling and duplicating cards that had been done by the day shift.' In other words, there was a day shift that called people to become block captains and you had people call the same people in the evening?

"MR. McMINOWAY: Yes, sir. They had stacks of cards similar to three by five index cards, and previous to the time I came over there the thing was not working very successfully, but I just stopped after that day—the cards that were there the day I came were the ones that were there the day I left. I never went to the stock room to get new supplies of cards.

"MR. DASH: But look at April 12th, it does not show a passive act, you wrote on April 12th: 'I rearranged the cards again that night shifts would re-call a lot of day shift cards.' I take it that is an accurate statement of what you did?

"MR. McMINOWAY: That is the way I read it, sir.

"MR. DASH: All right.

"Now, the impact and the effect of this repetitive calling you reflect in your diary on April 14th, and you write, 'Repetition of calls is starting to aggravate the volunteer block captains. The captains are getting called two or three times and it is beginning to bother them. Some captains have already quit because of the repeated calls.'

"So that this repetition did have a disruptive effect in getting block captains?

"MR. McMINOWAY: Do you want me to answer that?

"MR. DASH: Yes.

"MR. McMINOWAY: Yes, sir.

"MR. DASH: Actually, again on April 20th you state that 'We put some lists on the phone tables that had already been called so that repeat calls will be made tonight,' so this was continued again.

"Actually, this was quite a costly trouble for Mr. Humphrey because do you not indicate on April 11th that Mr. Humphrey was spending one-third of his budget on the phone bank and literature packets that the block captains would distribute?

"MR. McMINOWAY: This is the information that the Humphrey people had given me.

"MR. DASH: So that causing this disruption in terms of repeated calls and getting block captains to be annoyed and some quitting was taking quite a bite also out of the expense that Mr. Humphrey had allotted for the use of the phone banks. Is that true?

"MR. McMINOWAY: Yes, sir, it was.

"MR. DASH: You also, by the way, on April 22nd, wrote that you called, you yourself called people out of the Humphrey headquarters and urged them to vote for Jackson. You did do that?

"MR. McMINOWAY: Yes, sir.

"MR. DASH: That was three days right before the primary election. This is more than intelligence-gathering, is it not?

(Footnote 78 continued)

"MR. McMINOWAY: Yes, sir.

"MR. DASH: Your diary also indicates that you played a role in hiring persons for the phone bank in a later operation. What did you mean on April 18th in your diary when you state that you, you say 'I really lined up some winners.' What did you mean by winners?

"MR. McMINOWAY: Evidently these people were of low caliber qualifications.

"MR. DASH: Winners for you, losers for them, right?

"MR. McMINOWAY: Possibly.

"MR. DASH: On April 19th you wrote in your diary that 'went to the phone bank and checked on my workers as they were waiting for me at the door. I got them to separate the union and Negro cards into uneven rationed stacks. The 60 people lined up yesterday did not show up for work, only 24 came. The cards were so placed that anyone calling them could not distinguish between a Negro call sheet or a union call sheet. The call sheet is the speech read to the person called.'

"So as a result of that, I take it that some union people received a call that was directed to black voters and a black voter received a call directed to a union member?

"MR. McMINOWAY: In some instances.

"MR. DASH: I think also you were able, by the way, you managed, with all this, to win quite a bit of confidence in the Philadelphia headquarters.

"MR. McMINOWAY: Yes, sir. The jobs that I did with Miss Adcovitz and with the other staff members were always carried out to the best of my ability to be successful for the Humphrey candidacy, anything that I did that they specifically instructed me to do was done correctly.

"MR. DASH: I take it, from what we have just referred to on the phone bank, some of these things were not done to carry out successfully the Humphrey activities?

"MR. McMINOWAY: To put the situation into context, the phone bank situation was a mess when I got there. There was no proper supervision by the Humphrey staff conducted in that area. They spent a lot of money paying the expenses of the phone bank but they spent very little time supervising it and no real direct orders were given to the people working there as to the proper way of carrying it out. The phone bank system was new to me when I got there. I did use this opportunity to learn about it and so that in the future I would understand what this type of a setup was with the block captain."

For another example of harassment see testimony of Frank Mankiewicz, ibid., vol. 45 (mimeo.), pp. 9044-9045:

"There are a lot of examples of traditional Democratic leaders and labor people being phoned at embarrassing times with insulting messages and being told to be at a certain meeting which never took place. I am thinking particularly in New Jersey of a couple of times labor people in Jersey City and, I believe, in Newark, were called and peremptorily ordered to be at a meeting with Sargent Shriver at 8:00 o'clock in the morning, and they were called about 5:30 or 6:00 in the morning and told it was a McGovern coordinator calling and told to be at a meeting at 8:00 and, of course, a meeting was not scheduled, it had never been put on, it all contributed to a lot of bitterness in the Democratic Party.

"SENATOR MONTOYA: What about the call to President Meany of the AFL-CIO?

"MR. MANKIEWICZ: That call came prior to the Democratic Convention, about a week before. Somebody called to President Meany's secretary, asked to speak to Mr. Meany, was told that he was not there. The caller said, 'Well, this

(i) fraudulent use of the telephone to order food, supplies, and so on, for an opposition candidate; [79]

(j) causing the cancellation of speaking engagements and public appearances of an opposition candidate by phone; [80]

(Footnote 78 continued)

is Gary Hart, Senator McGovern's campaign manager, and if Mr. Meany knows what is good for him, he will be in New York tomorrow to meet with Senator McGovern.'

"It did not better relations with Mr. Meany and Senator McGovern. Indeed it embittered them."

See also testimony of Berl Bernhard, ibid., vol. 46 (mimeo.), pp. 9122-9123:

". . . of far greater significance were the literally hundreds, perhaps thousands, of phone calls which were made in the Manchester area of New Hampshire during the week-to-week-and-a-half prior to the primary. Callers identifying themselves as canvassers from the 'Harlem for Muskie Committee' urged the citizens to vote for Muskie because he would be 'so good for the black man.' These calls were being made between 12:00 at night and 3:00 a.m., in the morning. They did not strike me as advantageous. The black vote in New Hampshire may amount to one or two percent. But if it had amounted to 50 percent, it would still have hurt us. No one is favorably disposed toward any candidate who has people calling or appears to have people calling between 12:00 midnight and 3:00 in the morning. These calls resulted in many calls to me individually in Washington, D. C., complaining about our dumb campaign tactics, and they also resulted in calls from our campaign coordinator in New Hampshire, to see if there was any action I could take to stop them. The only thing I could think of doing was to call McGovern headquarters to tell them to cut it out. My recollection is that I spoke to Frank Mankiewicz, the McGovern political director, since I had assumed that the calls were McGovern-inspired. They denied that they had anything to do with this and the calls continued.

"The second part of the disruptive telephone strategy involved post-midnight calls from people alleging that they were canvassers for Muskie and asking how the people intended to vote. These calls apparently went beyond Manchester. I was informed that the recipients of these calls would sometimes receive three or four calls in rapid succession on the same evening. The source of all of these phone calls has never been uncovered, but I think it soured many people toward our campaign in New Hampshire."

[79] See testimony of Donald H. Segretti, ibid., vol. 41 (mimeo.), p. 8191:

"Senator Muskie was to have a fund-raising dinner at the Washington Hilton Hotel, and Mr. Kelly and I, ostensibly acting for Muskie Organizers, ordered flowers, pizzas, and liquor for the campaign workers."

[80] See ibid., p. 8221:

"MR. DASH: Now, was there an occasion when one of these infiltrators in Senator Muskie's campaign in Tampa leaked to the press that there was to be a secret $1,000 plate fund-raising dinner?

"MR. SEGRETTI: I believe that is correct.

"MR. DASH: Do you know what happened as a result of that leak?

"MR. SEGRETTI: I understand that the dinner which was to be attended by 17 individuals was subsequently cancelled.

"MR. DASH: Yes, and, therefore, the dinner was cancelled as a result of that information becoming public.

"MR. SEGRETTI: I heard that, yes, sir."

(k) distribution of misleading literature against a candidate without identifying the source; [81]

---

[81] See ibid., pp. 8221-8222:

"MR. DASH: Now, you have stated in your statement that you had various school busing posters printed up involving Mr. Muskie?

"MR. SEGRETTI: That is correct.

"MR. DASH: Would you look at tab 8. You will find at tab 8 in your series of exhibits because of the size of the poster it is somewhat broken up, but I think the poster read: 'Support busing now, support more children now.' [sic] I think I have a copy of this and you can see it. It says 'Help Muskie support busing more children now.' Is this the poster you are referring to?

"MR. SEGRETTI: That is correct, Mr. Dash.

"MR. DASH: And the reference in the bottom 'Mothers backing Muskie committee,' was that a committee that you made up?

"MR. SEGRETTI: Yes, sir. There is no committee by that name, to my knowledge."

See also, ibid., pp. 8224-8225:

"MR. DASH: Now, did your Florida agent distribute anti-Wallace cards purporting to be backing Mr. Muskie?

"MR. SEGRETTI: I believe Mr. Benz had some printed up and they were so distributed.

"MR. DASH: Would you take a look at tab 18. You will notice that part, I only direct your attention to the printed card: 'A vote for Wallace is a wasted vote; on March 14th cast your ballot for Senator Edmund Muskie.'

"Is that one of the cards?

"MR. DASH: If you turn the page, again looking at the printed part, the printed card 'If You Liked Hitler You'll Just Love Wallace.' Under this was 'Vote For Muskie.' Was that one of the cards?

"MR. SEGRETTI: No, sir.

(Conferring with counsel)

"I understand that the one—this was the same card printed on two sides?

"MR. DASH: Printed on two sides.

"MR. SEGRETTI: There was only one card, to my recollection.

"MR. DASH: Then, what I just read was on two sides of one card?

"MR. SEGRETTI: That is right."

And ibid., p. 8236:

"MR. DASH: Did you also have anti-Humphrey bumper stickers printed up?

"MR. SEGRETTI: I did have some.

"MR. DASH: Would you look at tab 20? I will just hold this up.

" 'Humphrey; he started the war; don't give him another chance; Democrats for Peace Candidate.'

"Is that one of the bumper stickers that you had printed up?

"MR. SEGRETTI: Yes.

"MR. DASH: By the way, that Democrats for Peace Candidate, what organization was that?

"MR. SEGRETTI: That was me again, Mr. Dash."

And ibid., pp. 8237-8239:

"MR. DASH: Now, did you also have a pamphlet printed up and distributed in California with regard to Mr. Humphrey? If you look at page 23, you can identify this pamphlet—tab 23.

"Now, that pamphlet shows a photograph of Senator Humphrey holding a bill fish, does it not?

(Footnote 81 continued)

"MR. SEGRETTI: That is correct.

"MR. DASH: And underneath the photograph is printed 'A fishy smell for the White House?'

"MR. SEGRETTI: That is correct.

"MR. DASH: And did you actually—this pamphlet looks very much like the earlier pamphlet that you identified, which was against Muskie, which had come out of the White House. You testified that you did not know it did, but it had been mailed to you and copied in about 5,000 copies.

"MR. SEGRETTI: That is right.

"MR. DASH: Was this dummied up from that pamphlet?

"MR. SEGRETTI: I thought the pamphlet I received relating to Senator Muskie was, seemed to be well done. I took that pamphlet and I patterned this pamphlet after it. The pictures I took from Time or Newsweek magazine.

"MR. DASH: And you have a picture inside of a UMW president, Tony Boyle, and a picture of Senator Humphrey, 'Memories of 1968—stop the bomb—end U.S. aggression.'

"Is that correct? If you will turn the page, you will see those photographs.

"MR. SEGRETTI: Yes.

"MR. DASH: And this particular pamphlet again repeats pretty much the language that was in the Senator Muskie pamphlet. 'Hubert H. Humphrey would be no different from the Nixons, Agnews, Mitchells, Reagans we have now.

" 'He is the "boss-candidate',' et cetera, and it is pretty derogatory of Senator Humphrey, is it not?

"MR. SEGRETTI: It is pretty much a copy of the same language that was in the pamphlet regarding Senator Muskie.

"MR. DASH: Well, this one seems to make Humphrey kind of a war-monger, does it not?

"MR. SEGRETTI: Well, I do not know if I would term it war-monger.

"MR. DASH: Well, also, it refers to him as a Democrat, a Democratic boss-candidate, does it not?

"MR. SEGRETTI: Yes, it does.

"MR. DASH: Apparently, the sponsor on this particular one, different from what appeared on the Muskie one, which said 'Democrats for a Liberal Alternative,' says 'Democrats Against Bossism.' T. Wilson, Chairman—is that again you?

"MR. SEGRETTI: That again, is a committee of one, me."

See also testimony of Berl Bernhard, ibid., vol. 46, pp. 9131-9132:

"Lest you assume that, and I hope you do not, that my comments are totally partisan, I should bring up a matter which hounded us in at least New Hampshire and that is the scurrilous and totally unjustified attacks upon Senator Muskie by one Stewart Mott.

"Mr. Mott financed a project early in 1972 consisting of various printed documents, with hand scrawled headlines written in red or black ink, and I have attached some of those copies of those delights to my statement. To say they constituted bad taste would enable me to exaggerate for the rest of my life and come out even. It accused Muskie's father of being a draft dodger. It included blatant falsehoods about Muskie's record and it was sent throughout the primary states beginning in New Hampshire. Segments of the larger pamphlets were run as full page newspaper ads which Mott financed. He even had the poor taste to send his diatribe to Mrs. Stephen Muskie, the Senator's daughter-in-law. There was similar outrageous material dealing with disclosure of campaign finances which he mailed to Senator Muskie's contributors—contributors whose addresses he was able to secure only because of the Senator's voluntary disclosure of his finances.

(Footnote 81 continued)

"I think it useless to refute each and every allegation because I would be here an even longer time. This material angered me toward the staff of Senator McGovern, because it was our belief, it was my belief, that Mr. Mott was a heavy contributor to McGovern. Therefore, we assumed that this was either being done at the behest of Senator McGovern or with his or their knowledge. As the campaign progressed, I called Frank Mankiewicz who swore he had nothing to do with this material.

"I should also note that the CREEP dirty tricks department found much favor in Mr. Mott's game and picked up on it. A Mott newspaper ad berating Senator Muskie on the financial disclosure issue was reprinted and distributed to those entering a Los Angeles Muskie fund-raising affair. At the bottom of the reprint were typed the words:

" 'The Committee will look for your names as part of Muskie's Fat Cats. They better be there.'

"We drew the natural conclusion that Mr. Mott was responsible for this harassment, although we have since learned that this was a Segretti ploy."

And see also testimony of Michael Heller, ibid., vol. 48 (mimeo.), pp. 9392-9394:

"MR. DASH: Would you finish the reading of that [pamphlet]?

"MR. HELLER: 'Senior Air Force Officials also indicated that if Mr. Nixon is re-elected without a negotiated settlement having been reached, the air war against North Vietnam would intensify.' Then it goes on. L.A. Times.

" 'Thanks to Modern Technology, Nixon Brings The Ovens To The People Rather Than The People To The Ovens.' Sponsored by the Jewish Campaign to End the Indochina Holocaust.

"MR. DASH: Do you know, is that an authentic organization, the Jewish Campaign to End the Indochina Holocaust? Do you know of it?

"MR. HELLER: To my knowledge, I have never heard of it before this flier.

"MR. DASH: Without in any way indicating the language of that last statement, Nixon brings the ovens to the people rather than the people to the ovens, was such a group to end the Indochina holocaust, would a fair interpretation at least be that it meant—perhaps bad judgment—to have meant the bombings or the use of napalm to be referred to by that statement? In other words, the purport of the statement?

"MR. HELLER: I don't know what the purport of the statement is.

"MR. DASH: All right. Where did you first see this leaflet?

"MR. HELLER: I first saw it in my office. Somebody had brought it in to my office and shown it to me.

"MR. DASH: What did you do about it then? Who brought it into your office?

"MR. HELLER: A volunteer worker.

"MR. DASH: A volunteer worker for whom?

"MR. HELLER: A volunteer worker who was working in my office.

"MR. DASH: For the—

"MR. HELLER: For the Democrats For Nixon.

"MR. DASH: All right. What did you do when you received this leaflet?

"MR. HELLER: When I received the leaflet, I didn't know what to think and I sent someone down, a volunteer—a volunteer had gone down to see if this was being handed out by the McGovern volunteers, and it was.

"MR. DASH: When you say it was, what did you see?

"MR. HELLER: Pardon me?

"MR. DASH: When you say, and it was, that is a conclusion. What did you see?

(l)   issuance of false press releases ostensibly on behalf of a candidate; [82] and

(m) paying for the display of public nudity, coupled with a showing of support for a candidate. [83]

(Footnote 81 continued)

"MR. HELLER: In other words, the volunteer came back to me and said that this piece of literature was being handed out in several places on the street, up and down the street between our office and the McGovern office.

"MR. DASH: And you said by McGovern workers?

"MR. HELLER: By people who my volunteer thought to be McGovern volunteers.

"MR. DASH: What did you do when you received that information?

"MR. HELLER: I had telephoned the person who was in charge of the press department for the Committee to Re-Elect. I told him about the piece of literature and I read him word for word everything on the literature. I told him that—he asked me if the McGovern people were handing it out? I told him that a volunteer had told me that they were.

"He told me to double check on it myself, which I did. I walked down the street. I saw people who I believed to be McGovern volunteer workers; I also saw this inside their headquarters. I did not go inside their headquarters, I saw it through the window.

"It has on the bottom, the Jewish Campaign to end the Indochina holocaust and no McGovern identification."

[82] See testimony of Martin D. Kelly, ibid., vol. 42 (mimeo.), pp. 8386-8387:

"MR. LENZNER: Did you also, with Mr. Segretti, issue false press releases?

"MR. KELLY: Yes, sir.

"MR. LENZNER: And again, for the same strategy, I take it?

"MR. KELLY: Yes, sir.

"MR. LENZNER: Can you describe briefly the nature of the releases, what they contained, if you remember them?

"MR. KELLY: I do not remember distinctly, I think one referred to Senator Humphrey. These were written on Muskie stationery. They referred to Senator Muskie's stand or at least claimed vague and ambiguous stand, of aid to Israel which, of course, did not go over very well in Miami Beach. I cannot recall exactly what the other, I think there were three releases, maybe four that I sent.

"MR. LENZNER: And that press release contrasted Senator Humphrey's position on that issue with Senator Muskie's to make it appear that it was a pamphlet or a flyer handed out by Senator Muskie?

"MR. KELLY: Yes."

[83] See ibid., p. 8434:

"SENATOR MONTOYA: I noticed that toward the last, you were planning on parading a nude woman past Muskie headquarters and she was supposed to shout, 'Muskie, I love you.'

"MR. KELLY: Well, that is not exactly the case. What was is there was a girl that was hungry for money. She needed some money, so I told her—I didn't know her. She was going to Gainesville, where the University of Florida is. I was told Senator Muskie was there. I gave her $20, $10, I don't remember how much, and asked her if I gave this to her if she would be willing to take off her clothes and run in front of his hotel, screaming, I love you—which she did, unfortunately.

"But she did.

"SENATOR MONTOYA: You must have known her very well.

Existing Law and Private Codes. Many such campaign tactics are already regulated by state and federal law [84] and are subject to a private code of fair campaign practices.

Under federal law, for example, it is illegal to distribute unsigned literature in the course of election campaigns for federal office. A federal statute provides:

> Whoever wilfully publishes or distributes or causes to be published or distributed . . . any card, pamphlet, circular, poster, dodger advertisement, writing, or other statement relating to or concerning any person who has publicly declared his intention to seek the office of President, Vice President . . ., or Senator or Representative . . . to Congress, in a primary, general, or special election, or convention of a political party . . ., which does not contain the names of the persons, associations, committees, or corporations responsible for the same . . . shall be fined not more than $1,000 or imprisoned not more than 1 year or both. [85]

Electronic surveillance of oral or wire communications of a candidate is also regulated by existing law. It is illegal to possess, manufacture or distribute wiretapping devices, as it is to intercept and subsequently disclose wire or oral communications. [86]

Numerous provisions of state laws are also applicable. A California statute, for example, regulates fraudulent telephone calls, [87] and burglary is a crime everywhere. In addition, there may be common law remedies (for instance, common law copyright) against those who remove or photocopy documents without permission. [88]

Finally, there is the Code of Fair Campaign Practices, a moral and ethical guide for the conduct of political campaigns. Although it has no legal sanctions, it condemns the

---

(Footnote 83 continued)

"MR. KELLY: Again unfortunately, no.

"SENATOR MONTOYA: How did you have so much confidence to ask her to do this?

"MR. KELLY: Well, it was more of a money thing as far as she was concerned. I certainly wouldn't approach somebody off—I shouldn't say off the street—off campus and offer to pay them $20 to strip and run in front of somebody's hotel, particularly around there. So I was very surprised that she would do this. I didn't expect it to happen, but it was just something that did happen."

[84] See note 70, Chapter 1, *supra.*

[85] 18 U.S.C., Section 612.

[86] 18 U.S.C., Sections 2512, 2511.

[87] California Penal Code, Section 474.

[88] See, for example, Nimmer on Copyright, Section 131.12.

(a) use of personal vilification, character defamation, . . . slander or scurrilous attacks on any candidate or personal or family life; (b) use of campaign material of any sort which misrepresents, distorts, or otherwise falsifies the facts regarding any candidate, as well as the use of malicious or unfounded accusations against any candidate which aim at creating or exploiting doubts, without justification, as to his loyalty and patriotism; . . . and (d) any dishonest or unethical practice which tends to corrupt or undermine our American system of free elections or which hampers or prevents the full and free expression of the will of the voters.[89]

Legislating against Dirty Tricks. A wholesale legislative assault on the "dirty tricks" problem would be unwise. The evidence before the Select Committee may have demonstrated the need for a statute relating to political espionage. This should be carefully drafted, requiring proof of specific intent, and should be limited to cases in which persons seek employment or remove or photocopy documents for purposes of political espionage. Beyond that need, however, substantial law already governs the most serious activities, and there are abundant pitfalls in undertaking its expansion.

There is the definitional problem of distinguishing the "dirty trick" from the harmless "prank." The hearings demonstrated a lack of general agreement. The distinction seems to depend almost entirely on whether the candidate one favors is the "hapless victim" or the "playful prankster." For example, many think that Dick Tuck's donning an engineer's cap and signaling a Nixon campaign train to pull out of the station as the candidate began to speak was a funny prank. It was also conduct designed to prevent a candidate from speaking to the public, no matter how great the residuum of humor or Mr. Tuck's willingness to take full public credit.[90]

---

[89] See S. Archibald, ed., *The Pollution of Politics* (Washington, D. C.: Public Affairs Press, 1971), pp. 8-9.

[90] See testimony of Patrick J. Buchanan, *Select Committee Hearings*, vol. 40 (mimeo.), pp. 8034-8035:

"MR. BUCHANAN: . . . . As you know Mr. Richard (Dick) Tuck is the well-known Democratic prankster. We enjoyed some of his tricks against us as well as, I am sure, he did. I recall in just three, briefly three of his favorites. One of them was in 1962 when Mr. Nixon began to deliver a major address from the back of a railroad train he put on an engineers cap and signaled the engineer to drive off leaving Mr. Nixon standing there.

"Another of his favorites was during a major political speech just as the speaker reaches the denouement he drops the fire escape on him.

There are further problems. A comprehensive statute will encounter serious constitutional problems. For example, any legislation attempting to regulate "smears," however desirable it may seem, will necessarily raise First Amendment questions under existing Supreme Court decisions. Even the federal statute prohibiting the distribution of unsigned campaign literature is subject to constitutional challenge,[91] for if there is value in political anonymity, weight must be accorded the need to engage in political dialogue without risking reprisals. Virtually any statute, moreover, must face the difficult constitutional problem of regulating heckling and demonstrations [92] which are as disruptive as naked girls, if less arresting. Whether a statute sufficiently narrow to survive constitutional attack is worth the drafting effort seems doubtful.

A comprehensive statute would entail yet a further risk. It would necessarily enable those in power to initiate prosecutions against their political enemies. One misleading aspect of Watergate is that it involved the criminality of incumbent officials, while new laws may have their greatest impact on challengers or losers. Indeed, the real lesson of the "enemies list" [93] may be "the less law the better." It would be another cruel irony to increase the power of incumbent officials to initiate political trials as a result of the revelations of Watergate.

One can hope, however, for movement in the direction of the voluntary regulation of dirty tricks. A joint congressional resolution might, for example, call upon the Republican and Democratic national chairmen to meet and discuss the "dirty tricks" problem with a view to agreeing upon a code to be incorporated in the platform of each party at its national convention. Such a code might establish private enforcement mechanisms similar to labor arbitration. Complaints of code violations might be submitted to an individual or panel for a decision by which the parties would agree to abide. The parties might further pledge that anyone who violated the code could not serve in

---

(Footnote 90 continued)

"The third was we were down at the Hotel Hilton down there in Miami Beach, and this was out front demonstrating there, I thought it was welfare mothers or we heard it was welfare mothers at the time, they were all black, they were all pregnant and they were all carrying placards that said 'Nixon's the one.' "

[91] Cf. Talley v. California, 362 U.S. 60 (1960).

[92] For an extensive textbook treatment of this complex problem, see Gerald Gunther and Noel T. Dowling, *Cases and Materials on Individual Rights in Constitutional Law* (Mineola, N.Y.: Foundation Press, Inc., 1970), pp. 554-626 and materials in *Supplements* thereto.

[93] See note 54, Chapter 1, *supra.*

any nonelective position within the party or in any national appointive office controlled by it.

Such a proposal risks being ineffective, but this is not inevitable. A congressional resolution would put the parties under considerable pressure to meet and reach agreement. The chances of this would be enhanced if the parties did not attempt to cover every abuse. For example, such a code would best avoid regulating the "smear" or "scurrilous" attack and concentrate on specific acts of sabotage or espionage such as those listed above. Once there was an agreement, the political pressure to abide by it would be considerable.

The suggestion does not provide watertight protection against unethical campaign tactics. It nevertheless creates political pressures in the right direction.

2

WATERGATE AND PRESIDENTIAL POWER

Executive Privilege

Part of the drama of Watergate arose from a series of struggles over the scope of the presidential privilege to withhold information from Congress and grand juries. Before the hearings, doubt existed as to whether President Nixon would instruct close aides not to testify on grounds of executive privilege.[1] In the event, the aides were permitted to testify. Upon the disclosure that almost all presidential conversations had been tape-recorded, litigation seeking production of the tapes followed. One action was brought by the special prosecutor, Archibald Cox, to compel production of certain tapes for the grand jury investigating the Watergate affair. Another action was brought by the Select Committee's suit to compel production of many of the same tapes. The grand jury subpoena partially succeeded, in that the Court of Appeals for the District of Columbia ordered the recordings produced for *in camera* inspection by Judge Sirica to determine whether they should go to the grand jury.[2] The committee's action was dismissed by Judge Sirica on the grounds that he lacked jurisdiction to enforce congressional subpoenas.[3] Subsequently, Congress passed a statute, which the President neither signed nor vetoed, em-

---

[1] See, for example, the statement of then Attorney General Richard G. Kleindienst, *Hearings before the Subcommittee on Intergovernmental Relations of the Committee on Government Operations and the Subcommittees on Separation of Powers and Administrative Practice and Procedure of the Committee on the Judiciary, United States Senate*, 93rd Congress, 1st session (1973), p. 30.

[2] Nixon v. Sirica (D. C. Cir., decided October 12, 1973), Civil Nos. 73-1962, 73-1967, and 73-1989.

[3] Senate Select Committee on Presidential Campaign Activities v. Nixon (D.D.C., decided October 17, 1973), Civil Action No. 1593-73.

powering the District Court for the District of Columbia to enforce the Select Committee's subpoenas.[4] A massive demand for documents and tapes followed, and further litigation appears inevitable.

Although the Select Committee's charter did not instruct it to investigate executive privilege,[5] the privilege is intimately related to the problem of crime detection in the executive branch and the hearings raised a question whether Congress ought to legislate in this area.

The Scope of Executive Privilege. The threshold question is whether any privilege should be recognized. Some have argued that such a prerogative lacks a historical or constitutional basis.[6] That early precedents seem more limited than present claims and that the Constitution itself mentions no such privilege cannot be denied. Nevertheless, the power to maintain confidentiality in particular circumstances has been repeatedly asserted by Presidents and their subordinates[7] (not to mention the Founding Fathers who wrote the Constitution in secret session) and the "expounding" of a constitution is not a process wholly dependent on explicit language. From the beginning it has been recognized that a constitution cannot employ the "prolixity of a legal code" to describe governmental powers because "its nature . . . requires that only its great outlines should be marked, its important objects designated, and the minor ingredients . . . deduced from the

---

[4] S. 2641, 93rd Congress, 1st session, reprinted in the *Congressional Record*, December 3, 1973, p. H 10484, approved by the House of Representatives on that date, thus clearing it for action by the President.

[5] It was, however, realized early on that executive privilege would be considered. See Opening Statement by Senator Ervin, *Select Committee Hearings*, Phase I, Book 1, p. 2.

[6] Raoul Berger, "Executive Privilege v. Congressional Inquiry," *UCLA Law Review*, vol. 12 (1965), p. 1044 and p. 1287, and the subsequent discussion. *Contra*, see Younger, "Congressional Investigations and Executive Secrecy: A Study in the Separation of Powers," *University of Pittsburgh Law Review*, vol. 20 (1959), p. 755.

[7] See, for example, summary of the arguments made before the Supreme Court, reported with the Court's opinion in Marbury v. Madison, 5 U.S. (1 Cranch) 137 (1803). Levi Lincoln, then attorney general, "having been summoned, and now called, objected to answering. . . . On the one hand, he respected the jurisdiction of this court, and on the other, he felt himself bound to maintain the rights of the executive . . . his objections were of two kinds. 1st. He did not think himself bound to disclose his official transactions while acting as secretary of state; and 2nd. He ought not to be compelled to answer anything which might tend to criminate himself," ibid., pp. 143–144. The Court said that Lincoln was bound to answer because nothing confidential need be disclosed, but that "if he [Lincoln] thought that anything was communicated to him in confidence, he was not bound to disclose it; nor was he obliged to state anything which would criminate himself," ibid., p. 144.

nature of the objects themselves."[8] Resort to implications drawn from the nature of the presidential office and its powers,—or as Charles L. Black would put it, from "structure and relationship"[9]—is thus a perfectly legitimate method of determining and defining executive privilege.

Some, concerned about secrecy in government, believe little or no privilege ought to attach to information or documents in the executive branch.[10] They believe the denial of privilege will increase the public's capacity to evaluate and influence decisions within the executive branch and thus expose decision makers to a wider range of opinions than they might otherwise encounter.

This argument seems overstated, however. While a denial of any such privilege and an aggressive pursuit of data may for a time increase the information available to the public, this may be a temporary phenomenon. The desire for confidentiality cannot be outlawed, and members of the executive branch can adjust their affairs in a way which decreases the anticipated gain and weakens the decision-making process. Pentagon studies do not have to be written, conversations do not have to be recorded, and advice does not have to be committed to paper. But this would be at a cost to the efficiency and rationality of the decision-making process.

The quality of deliberations may also decline. Advisors may mute the sharpness of their views if they are concerned about how their advice will look in the morning papers, and "risky" proposals will be avoided, as will even modest attempts at devil's advocacy. There is, finally, considerable pressure on any administration to conceal divisions within its ranks, and a lack of privacy can only increase the pressure to weed out those with conflicting viewpoints, thus further diminishing the quality of internal debate.

The "sunlight" of disclosure may, in addition, reduce flexibility by hardening initial positions taken in the course of deliberations or negotiations. Whether it be the Founding Fathers or the Arabs and Israelis, delicate political problems cannot be peacefully resolved if every idea presented, every word spoken, or every bargain offered is immediately transmitted abroad. The lack of privacy may thus be

---

[8] McCulloch v. Maryland, 17 U.S. (4 Wheat.) 316, 407 (1819).

[9] Charles L. Black, Jr., *Structure and Relationship in Constitutional Law* (Baton Rouge: Louisiana State University Press, 1969).

[10] See, for example, H.R. 6438, 93rd Congress, 1st session, reprinted in "Availability of Information to Congress," *Hearings before a Subcommittee on Government Operations, House of Representatives*, 93rd Congress, 1st session (1973), p. 12. See also the statement by the bill's sponsor, Mr. Fascell, reprinted in ibid., p. 156.

more characteristic of a politics of confrontation than of a politics of compromise.

In fact, the very nature of representative government would seem to call for an executive privilege of some scope. Although the American system of representation has not been placed taxonomically with any precision, it does incorporate many of the finer aspects of the Burkean model.[11] The decisions of the representative, whether a member of Congress or the President, are public and he is accountable for them. He is not, however, a mirror for the momentary views of his constituents. A considerable amount of independent judgment and thoughtful deliberation is expected and the result must be defended at the risk of losing office. Since it is the representative's responsibility to make the final judgment, he should also have discretion to determine what decisional procedures he will employ, with whom he will consult, and, if he chooses, to surround these processes with privacy. The no-privacy model seems more a part of a system of continual national referenda than of representative government.

Some form of executive privilege should, therefore, be recognized. This does not mean, however, as has been suggested, that it encompasses every bit of information possessed by the President which he believes cannot be published without damage to the national interest.[12] The scope of executive privilege, implied as it is from the nature of the presidential office, can cover only subject matters fairly related to the exercise of the functions and powers of that office, not to a particular President's idea of what is in the national interest at a particular time.

Since the President has primacy in negotiating with foreign governments, he may preserve the confidentiality of such negotiations.[13] So too, as commander-in-chief of the armed forces, he can impose secrecy on the grounds of military necessity.[14] Similar considerations apply to internal discussions undertaken with a view to the appoint-

---

[11] Hannah F. Pitkin, *The Concept of Representation* (Berkeley: University of California Press, 1967), pp. 168-189.

[12] The position was set out in an Attorney General's Memorandum, reprinted in *Hearings before the Subcommittee on Constitutional Rights of the Senate Judiciary Committee on Freedom of Information and Secrecy in Government*, 85th Congress, 2d session (1958), p. 33.

[13] See testimony of former Secretary of State Dean Acheson, *Hearings before the Subcommittee on Separation of Powers of the Committee on the Judiciary, United States Senate*, 92nd Congress, 1st session (1971), p. 259 (hereinafter referred to as *Hearings on Executive Privilege*).

[14] See statement of then Assistant Attorney General William H. Rehnquist in ibid., p. 432.

ment of federal officers, to the fulfilling of his responsibility to "take Care that the Laws be faithfully executed," [15] or other legitimate exercises of presidential power.

Many have asserted that executive privilege does not encompass the withholding of politically embarrassing material solely because it is embarrassing. [16] This, however, is an overstatement, for while the fact that material may be embarrassing does not bring it within the privilege, a quite proper motive for invoking privilege is to avoid embarrassment. Indeed, it is precisely to prevent the fear of embarrassment from impeding negotiations with foreign nations or from deterring candid advice that a privilege of confidentiality is recognized.

Many have also asserted that executive privilege does not cover "political" matters such as election strategies and the like. [17] This may be the case but is of little practical significance, since government inquiry into political activity is almost surely limited by the First Amendment, [18] a point perhaps easier to appreciate if the case is turned around and the demands for information are directed at a candidate challenging an incumbent President.

Further definition of the scope of the privilege in this paper seems unwise. Much turns on the particular facts at issue and the question is not in any event readily answered by resort to our legal system.

The Weight of the Privilege. Executive privilege is put in a misleading context when treated solely as a problem of law, for it is not an area in which precise legal rules are either desirable or possible. If it were established, for example, that the President possessed an extremely broad executive privilege, holders of that office would invoke it more frequently since the political cost of doing so is less once the law "legitimates" it. Similarly, where the courts give Congress access to materials in the executive branch, resort to the courts to get information will be more frequent and abuses will inevitably occur.

Either result is thus bad, but there is little middle ground apart from a series of essentially ad hoc decisions. The reason for this is that in a large body of cases no ascertainable weight can be assigned

---

[15] U.S. Constitution, Article II, Section 3.

[16] See, for example, testimony of William H. Rehnquist, *Hearings on Executive Privilege before the Subcommittee on Separation of Powers of the Committee on the Judiciary, United States Senate*, 92nd Congress, 1st session (1971), p. 422.

[17] See, for example, statement of Senator Ervin, *Select Committee Hearings*, Phase I, Book 5, p. 1864: ". . . I don't think that executive privilege covers any political activities whatsoever. They are not official and have no relation to his office."

[18] Cf. NAACP v. Alabama, 357 U.S. 449 (1958).

to the "need" to know or the "need" for privacy. In a particular conflict over access to information, the "needs" are determined as much by the political circumstances as by general principles of government. For example, congressional demands for information usually result as much from a desire to make political gains through exposure for exposure's sake as from a concern that legislation rest on adequate factual data. Similarly, presidential resistance will be generated as much by a fear of adverse public opinion or misunderstanding as by a desire to protect the quality of executive decision making. The problem with applying "law" to such cases is that it ignores the political aspects (exposure versus fear of adverse public reaction or misunderstanding) and concentrates solely on the "legal" aspects (legislative purposes versus protection of decision-making processes). A court cannot, for example, "weigh" whether exposure of certain facts at a particular time is irresponsible, or that the facts exposed are in the particular context misleading. Nor can it "weigh" whether a President is engaged in a "cover up" or just waiting until a complete recital of all the facts can be given the public. The political aspects, however, are legitimate, if not "legal," and some respect must be shown them if we are to have a sensible political process. Exposure has a place, as does allowing officials to have a say in the timing and manner in which the exposure comes about.

Both the "need" for confidentiality and the "need" to know thus depend in many cases largely on how politically relevant, or embarrassing, the particular material is. Political accommodation is the most appropriate way to resolve such conflicts, for it realistically tests the asserted "needs" and yet permits the public to get as much as or as little information as it believes desirable. The "secrecy" issue is no more subject to a single principled resolution than is the question of tax rates. The ultimate decision belongs with the people and excessive reliance upon the judicial process is likely to decrease public sensitivity to its own responsibilities.

This is not to dismiss any role for law, for as the need for the information seems more and more specific, the ability to weigh conflicting claims as a matter of law grows. This point is best demonstrated by comparing congressional subpoenas with those of a grand jury.

Congressional Subpoenas. Where Congress is seeking information from the executive, no general statute governing judicial enforcement of subpoenas seems appropriate, other than a statute authorizing enforcement where information has been withheld but the President has not himself specifically invoked executive privilege.[19] Hearings in Congress have demonstrated that lower officials in the bureaucracy frequently withhold information from Congress on grounds of executive privilege without specific authorization from the President.[20] That a genuine need for confidentiality exists should not be determined at that level and such claims are not entitled to the respect given presidential invocations of the privilege. It might be argued that since the privilege is the President's to assert, he can determine who may invoke it and may delegate it to subordinate officials. Coordinate branches such as the courts and Congress, however, need not recognize a delegation which reduces the political visibility of the use of the privilege. For, if political accommodation is the goal and the primary test of an assertion of the privilege is its political viability, the President ought not escape the political cost of invoking the privilege by delegating it to a subordinate official.

A general statute empowering the courts to enforce all congressional subpoenas seems unwise, particularly if it were to establish jurisdiction to enforce subpoenas issued by a committee, for that would invite abuse by small numbers of congressmen. Such a statute should at least require that the whole body vote the subpoena.

A more general statute also seems undesirable, however, for the usual congressional probe raises issues which are not fit for judicial resolution. Most such cases have political concerns at their core, with one side seeking political advantage from disclosure while the other resists or seeks to control disclosure so that its actions appear in the best light. No one familiar with the workings of the Congress doubts that the very decision to hold hearings is essentially political.

For reasons stated above, these political forces should not be disregarded, yet the judiciary must do just that when they weigh only "legal" claims, that is, legislative purpose versus the need for confidentiality. This, however, is to decide an abstraction, to resolve a case which has no resemblance to the real issues. It is, in short, nonjusticiable and should be so treated by the courts, thus denying compulsory process to the Congress in most cases. This, of course, is a legal victory for the executive, albeit on grounds which avoid taking a position on the merits of the claim of executive privilege.

---

[19] For a suggestion that the President himself be required to invoke the privilege (whatever its scope) see S. 1125, 92nd Congress, 1st session, introduced by Senator Fulbright, reprinted in *Hearings on Executive Privilege*, p. 8.

[20] See testimony of J. W. Fulbright, in ibid., p. 18 ff. and that of William P. Bundy, ibid., p. 317 ff.

This may seem to give too little power to Congress to get information from the executive, but Congress has considerable power to impose political costs upon a recalcitrant executive. It can fail to pass legislation in the absence of what it believes is relevant information, fail to confirm appointments in cases where data is withheld, and provide in legislation establishing programs that they are to be suspended if certain information about their execution is not turned over to Congress.[21] There is, moreover, a political cost in public opinion a President must pay if he appears to be concealing relevant information. Finally, Congress may openly retaliate against the President—by cutting off funds for certain staff, for example—if strongly desired information is withheld. If the courts take the position that such disputes are non-justiciable rather than holding that a broad executive privilege exists, the legislative retaliation would not be open to the constitutional challenge that it violates the separation of powers. The Congress is thus not impotent when it comes to enforcing its wishes against claims of executive privilege, and political accommodation is usually a viable means of resolving such conflict. Congress's power will depend largely upon its ability to mobilize public opinion behind its demands.

There may be a class of cases, however, in which a very specific legislative need for information exists, and legislation authorizing enforcement of subpoenas is proper. Such circumstances exist when legislative action in fact turns on the existence or nonexistence of a particular fact. The paradigm case would seem to be subpoenas issued in the course of impeachment proceedings which seek specific information relating to the commission of impeachable offenses. Here the legislative need seems easier to weigh (though political considerations abound) because the investigation has quite precise goals established for it. Before enforcing such subpoenas, a court must determine that a genuine impeachment inquiry is involved and that probable cause for such an investigation exists. Enforcement should be granted only when the need for the information outweighs the damage to the executive's decisional processes and when safeguards are adopted similar to those which should attach to enforcement of grand jury subpoenas (see below). Whether this reasoning can be extended to other legislative action is not clear but by no means foreclosed. Congress should, however, forgo resort to compulsory process except

---

[21] This course has apparently been adopted with regard to agencies dealing in foreign affairs; Arthur M. Schlesinger, *The Imperial Presidency* (Boston: Houghton Mifflin Co., 1973), pp. 395-400.

where a specific and genuine legislative need can be demonstrated, cases in which legislative action in fact turns on the information.

Grand Jury Subpoenas. Where grand juries are concerned, different considerations apply. When an investigation of a particular crime is involved, the need for evidence—for example, relevance, the existence of alternative sources—can be more easily weighed against the undesirable impact of disclosure. Indeed, this is precisely the kind of determination courts traditionally make. The power to retaliate politically, moreover, does not exist where grand juries seek evidence, and resolution of conflicts through political accommodation is not a realistic alternative. Only the "slippery slope" argument that such inquiries cannot be contained, either in scope of material sought or in maintaining the confidentiality of material obtained, can justify a claim of absolute privilege. Although this is a real difficulty, safeguards can be provided to prevent abuse in the very occasional case that will arise.

Legislation is desirable. Overlooked in the tapes litigation was the lack of a statute explicitly authorizing subpoenas of material in the possession of the President and covered by executive privilege. Although the argument was not made, there is a body of case law suggesting that statutes be construed to avoid constitutional issues where a legitimate choice exists between one interpretation with constitutional implications and another without. The purpose of the doctrine has been said to be to ensure that other branches of government fulfill their constitutional responsibilities by explicitly stating their view of a particular constitutional problem before the courts undertake to resolve it.[22] If such a canon of construction is valid, it might call for the quashing of a grand jury subpoena to the President, since there has been no explicit decision by Congress that such a confrontation over executive privilege is either desired or appropriate. Indeed, the only authority for the subpoenas seems to be the Federal Rules of Criminal Procedure, drafted by the Supreme Court and effective only by reason of Congress's failure to veto them, a process in which no explicit attention was given to executive privilege and the President had no opportunity to exercise his constitutional power of the veto.[23]

The statute should be carefully drawn, however, and contain appropriate safeguards. In general, it should "track" the court of appeals decision in the tapes case.[24] It should require *sworn testimony*

---

[22] Alexander M. Bickel, *The Least Dangerous Branch* (Indianapolis: Bobbs-Merrill, 1964), p. 164 et seq.

[23] 18 U.S.C., Sections 3771-3772.

[24] Nixon v. Sirica (D. C. Cir., decided October 12, 1973), Civil Nos. 73-1962, 73-1967, and 73-1989.

that *specifically described* evidence is *relevant* to a criminal investigation and *otherwise unobtainable* as well as a factual finding that *probable cause* to believe a crime has been committed exists. The court should then review the evidence *in camera* to determine whether the need for disclosure outweighs whatever harm it may do, to excise intermingled and irrelevant material, and to delete superfluous or embarrassing phrases and the like.

Presidential Acts in the Name of Domestic or National Security

The "Plumbers," the so-called Kissinger taps, the Huston plan and other activities have raised the question of presidential power to act without congressional authority in the name of domestic or national security as a central issue in the complex affair called Watergate. To the extent such inherent power exists, it flows from three sources: (1) the President's power as commander-in-chief, (2) his primary role in the execution of foreign policy, and (3) his responsibility to execute the laws.

Domestic Security. Under present law, presidential power to act in the name of domestic security without statutory authority seems minimal.[25] Where there is no foreign involvement, for example, the Supreme Court has required compliance with the usual wiretap prerequisites of a warrant,[26] a holding strongly indicating (if not establishing *a fortiori*) that break-ins and the like are subject to the usual legal rules. This is not to deny emergency power in the presidency, but to limit it to a truly complete collapse of law and government.[27] Only then are the normal methods of law enforcement, subject to the usual constitutional restraints, inadequate to preserve constitutional rule. In such extreme circumstances, the President is the only officer of the government capable of retrieving the situation, restoring constitutional rule, and preserving legitimacy. As Mr. Justice Jackson put it, the Bill of Rights ought not be read as a suicide pact.[28]

---

[25] For instance, the Supreme Court has essentially rejected the contention that the President has inherent power as commander-in-chief to act in domestic affairs, absent any constitutionally valid statutory authority; Youngstown Sheet & Tube Co. v. Sawyer, 343 U.S. 579 (1952).

[26] United States v. United States District Court, 407 U.S. 297 (1972).

[27] Thus, even commentators skeptical of the national or domestic security rationale qualify their assertions in this regard. See, "Note, Developments in the Law, the National Security Interest and Civil Liberties," *Harvard Law Review*, vol. 85 (1972), p. 1259. See also "Note, Honored in the Breach: Presidential Authority to Execute the Laws with Military Force," *Yale Law Journal*, vol. 83 (1973), p. 130.

[28] Jackson, J. (dissenting), Terminiello v. Chicago, 337 U.S. 1, 37 (1949).

The primary incentive for domestic security operations is intelligence gathering. Once illegal activities by the groups or individuals in question occur, the normal channels of domestic law enforcement can be brought to bear. The risk in permitting before-the-fact wiretapping and the like (apart from the invasion of privacy involved) lies in the inevitable temptation to amass investigatory data for purposes other than the detection or prevention of crime. Harassment of political opponents, destruction of reputations, and perhaps even physical violence may seem viable and attractive ways to proceed. Limiting the range of permissible action admittedly entails the risk of being unable to prevent violent acts. Nonetheless, the increase of legitimacy of the government and the higher level of trust in the society that a limited inherent domestic security power carries probably outweigh its risks.[29]

National Security. The law may be more permissive where there is foreign involvement. Where, for example, the President is acting "to protect the Nation against actual or potential attack or other hostile acts of a foreign power, to obtain foreign intelligence information deemed essential to the security of the United States, or to protect national security information against foreign intelligence activities,"[30] wiretapping without a warrant may be permissible, although this has yet to be authoritatively established.

There is reason, however, to distinguish domestic security cases from those in which foreign involvement exists. There are no international instrumentalities responsible for the functions performed by domestic law enforcement agencies and, unlike the case of domestic security, no reason to suppose less shadowy alternatives are available. Moreover, covert operations and espionage seem characteristic of major powers. While the case for prohibiting all such activities by the United States government on American soil has merit, the fact that adversary governments do not so limit themselves creates a heavy presumption against those who would deny such tactics to their own government.

The need for secrecy is great because of the very nature of the operations. Moreover, even where every government involved knows of them, reasons for continued secrecy exist. Diplomatic accommoda-

---

[29] One scholar has stated the concept of legitimacy in this fashion: " . . . legitimacy comes to a regime that is felt to be good and to have proven itself as such to generations past as well as in the present. Such a government must be principled as well as responsible. . . ." Alexander M. Bickel, *The Least Dangerous Branch*, p. 29.

[30] 18 U.S.C., Section 2511(3).

tions may depend on the respective governments' maintaining silence about the covert activities in which they are mutually engaged.[31]

New Legislation. Actions in the name of national security entail decisions based on considerations both of great urgency and great delicacy. Of necessity they must be judged after the fact, and legal limitations are likely to be perceived by responsible officials more as a factor raising the political stakes than as effective denials of power. What law can do most effectively, therefore, is raise what Alexander Bickel has called the "threshold" for taking such actions.[32]

The greater risk for society may be in restraints on government which both the people and officialdom find unreasonable than in permitting leeway where the need seems most compelling. Modern governments may inevitably resort to electronic surveillance or similar intrusions when they believe their security is at stake. If so, a wholesale prohibition will never work, and may, by treating different activities as equally impermissible, actually encourage the least desirable kind of conduct. In such circumstances, the soundest strategy may be to concentrate on stopping the least desirable while channelling the most acceptable into regularized procedures.

Several possible changes in existing law deserve consideration. First, the recent Supreme Court decision that the President does not have inherent power to authorize domestic security wiretaps[33] raises the question whether Congress should legislate regarding the issuance of warrants in such cases. Wiretapping is now permitted upon a showing of probable cause for crimes involving atomic secrets, espionage, sabotage, treason, injury to the person of the President or a member of Congress, riots, and conspiracies to commit any of these crimes.[34] To augment this authority would effectively do away with the probable cause requirement. Increases in the intelligence gathering capabilities of federal law enforcement agencies must be at the cost of authorizing taps whenever those agencies believe a group or individual is inclined

---

[31] An analogous example of the need for continued secrecy exists in the case of the President's decision to withhold from Congress information about a completed treaty negotiation. See testimony of William H. Rehnquist in *Hearings on Executive Privilege*, p. 430. While this may seem simply an abstract exercise in international relations game theory, the practice of mutual non-revelation is probably widespread. Indeed, that it is broken only in the most extreme circumstances tends to corroborate the hypothesis.

[32] Alexander M. Bickel, "Watergate and the Legal Order," *Commentary*, January 1974, p. 23.

[33] United States v. United States District Court, 407 U.S. 297 (1972).

[34] 18 U.S.C., Section 2516.

to engage in activities thought to threaten domestic security. Requiring a belief as to inclination, moreover, may in practice be no restraint at all. That the benefits outweigh the costs seems problematic at best.

Were such wiretaps to be given statutory sanction—this is not recommended here—a requirement that warrants be sought only on the explicit written authorization of the President should be imposed and any wiretap not so authorized made illegal. If the President cannot disavow taps which misfire politically while his subordinates claim to have been acting legally, the "threshold" will be raised and political harassment and espionage will be at great risk.

Incipiency is more serious in foreign than in domestic affairs, and the need for preventive action or the gathering of intelligence is considerably greater. Still, an attempt to define presidential power with precision will inevitably be either too constraining or too easily used to justify unwarranted actions against American citizens. The solution is to be found in increasing the political risks of misuse but leaving operational decisions to the President.

It has been argued that the wiretapping of foreign embassies is far more likely to intrude on the privacy of unsuspecting United States citizens than on sophisticated employees of foreign governments,[35] but the invasion of privacy seems rather small when measured against what is at stake in foreign affairs. To require a warrant in such cases would impose a troublesome and anomalous requirement. How probable cause can be established without risking embarrassment to our relations with other governments is not at all clear. Of what, moreover, must probable cause be shown? Such inappropriate requirements, one suspects, would merely lead to the rubber stamping of warrants.

One suggestion may make more sense. At present, national security wiretaps require the signature only of the attorney general of the United States. He does not seem, however, the most appropriate official to make the sole judgment. The alleged benefits are in the area of foreign and military affairs, where he has little concern, while the risks lie in the unwarranted extension into domestic matters, the area of his principal responsibility. Authority for actions taken in the name of national security, therefore, should be located in other officials in addition to the attorney general. Congress, or the President by executive order, might require that such wiretaps be undertaken only if specifically authorized by (besides the attorney general) the President or by the secretary of state *and* the secretary of defense, officials

---

[35] "Note, Developments in the Law, the National Security Interest and Civil Liberties," *Harvard Law Review*, vol. 85 (1972), p. 1267.

with responsibility in the particular areas. This will impose restraint on the expansionary proclivities one may find in an official charged with domestic law enforcement and decrease the possibility that wire-tapping will be undertaken without good cause. This imposes no great hardship if in fact there is a need for such activities. Under no circum-stances should the authority be lodged in members of the White House staff, whose own responsibilities are diffuse and whose authority to speak for the President is unclear.

Finally, Congress might consider designating certain high execu-tive branch positions as so sensitive to national security that wire-tapping of those holding them is permitted at any time. This is a suggestion made here with little confidence in its merit but out of the apprehension that such tapping will occur anyway and the hope that a line recognizing the inevitable will increase the political penalties for wholly unjustified expansions of what is necessary for "security." While many officials doubtless now expect (and may accept the fact) they will be tapped, the proposal does have the merit of erasing doubt and warning all, including those who may call these officials, that a limited invasion of privacy is permissible.

Political Control and Democratic Responsiveness: The Department of Justice

Partisan Influence and Electoral Control. Because the Watergate hear-ings and related investigations disclosed so many allegations of abuse of executive power for partisan purposes, many observers concluded that executive agencies need more "independence" from political con-trol. If the director of the FBI destroys files which may embarrass the administration politically, if Justice Department investigations into Watergate seem inadequate, or if Internal Revenue Service investiga-tory decisions are vulnerable to White House pressure, the natural remedy may seem to be a loosening of White House control. Typical of such proposals is Senator Ervin's bill to establish the Department of Justice as an independent agency outside the executive branch, with the attorney general serving a six-year term.[36]

This proposal demonstrates both the merits and costs of dimin-ishing political control. As Senator Ervin said when he introduced the legislation,

---

[36] S. 2803, 93rd Congress, 1st session; see Press Release, Subcommittee on Separa-tion of Powers, Committee on the Judiciary, United States Senate, "Ervin Intro-duces Bill to Create Independent Department of Justice," December 12, 1973, Washington, D. C.

A cornerstone of our system of justice is the faith of the American people in that system and their belief in its fairness. Even the appearance of impropriety or unfairness undermines faith in that system. For this reason, Congress should now thoroughly review the duties and functions of the Department of Justice and take action to insure that it is independent of political influence. The Department of Justice should be insulated from the direct political control of the Executive Branch of government to preserve the independence essential to the proper administration of Justice.[37]

The worthiness of any proposal to limit the use of the Department of Justice as a partisan instrument can hardly be denied. Political control, however, implies more than partisan direction and its elimination may be at a great cost in the loss of democratic control over a critical instrument of government.

Consider the many areas for which the Justice Department has responsibility: the FBI, local law enforcement assistance, antitrust enforcement, many civil actions involving the government, federal criminal law enforcement, judicial appointments, federal prisons, civil rights enforcement, immigration, representation of the government in the Supreme Court, to name a few.[38] Only if infinite resources are available can the department undertake to perform every function that conceivably falls within its jurisdiction. Federal law itself, moreover, is not a tight system of rules, each of which is enforced to the hilt in every possible circumstance. Even after the decision to commit resources to an area is made, important questions of policy remain.

Decisions as to priorities are thus essential. For example, should more or less of the department's resources be devoted to enforcing laws aimed at organized crime, to civil rights efforts, or to enforcement of the Internal Revenue Code? What resources should go to programs designed to aid urban law enforcement agencies? To what extent should the department act vigorously in areas in which federal and state law overlap? What should antitrust policy be?

If the Department of Justice is "independent," the priorities will presumably be fixed by the attorney general who, because he can neither be fired not instructed by the President, will be only indirectly responsible to the electorate. The solution of "independence" does tend to eliminate partisan pressure from the White House, but only by lessening electoral control over an important agency of government. The allocation of scarce resources among civil rights, urban

---

[37] Ibid.

[38] 28 U.S.C., Section 501 et seq.

crime and antitrust enforcement, however, seems preeminently a question for the political process, to be resolved by persons who are politically accountable rather than "independent."

Indeed, that "independence" will actually eliminate partisan influence is no certainty, for while presidential control can be diminished, others will almost surely find their power increased. An "independent" attorney general, after all, can be consumed with personal political ambition. It would also be anomalous to separate the Department of Justice from presidential control only to shift it in part to the chairmen of the congressional judiciary committees or private "client" groups of the department. Because such a shift will be to persons or groups with relatively narrow constituencies, their influence will likely be exercised on behalf of very special interests.

The dilemma is, therefore, that the risk of partisan abuse cannot be eliminated without severely lessening democratic control. Power can always be put to uses other than those intended and an administration willing to abuse its powers systematically can never be fully controlled. While expectations of reform must be adjusted downward, they need not be abandoned. Some reforms attempted in the past, however, can be rejected. Congressional oversight committees, for example, seem of relatively little value in deterring agencies from wrongful behavior and may well have the very undesirable effect of falsely reassuring Congress and the public.[39] On the other hand, the Senate can reject appointments in the Department of Justice which by their nature threaten to increase partisan influence. While the attorney general should be political in his conception of the proper ordering of departmental priorities and policies, and the President ought thus to have considerable discretion in choosing men whose views coincide with his own, the attorney general need hardly be a partisan political warrior. The appointment of a presidential campaign manager to the post of attorney general, a frequent practice of both parties,[40] greatly increases the risks, particularly since he may have responsibilities looking to reelection. The Senate, nevertheless, has routinely confirmed campaign managers.

Lines of communication between the White House staffers, the attorney general, and lesser officials in the Department of Justice ought to be clarified. When presidential assistants of various rank can routinely call around the department with inquiries and directives of a

---

[39] See, for example, Kenneth C. Davis, *Administrative Law Treatise* (St. Paul, Minn.: West Publishing Co., 1958), vol. 1, section 6.08.

[40] In recent times, the list includes J. Howard McGrath (Truman), Herbert Brownell (Eisenhower), Robert F. Kennedy (Kennedy), and John Mitchell (Nixon).

sensitive nature,[41] the least responsible person in the White House may be able to influence decisions in the department, and its officials become less accountable for their actions. Administration control need not be diminished but merely routed through specified channels.

The exercise of discretionary authority in matters of particular litigation raises more difficult problems. While matters of general policy must be resolved by political judgments, individual cases should be disposed of according to general policy and not according to the political influence of a litigant. This does not mean that the disposition of particular litigation should be separated from political control, for questions of settlement, plea bargaining and consent decrees can raise important policy issues. What is called for are devices which preserve that control but deter the exercise of improper influence.

Attorney General Richardson directed that records be kept of all calls and visits (from within government and without) relating to particular cases so that improper approaches would be discouraged.[42] This practice should be continued. Also worthy of consideration is establishment of a routine in which individual cases are not discussed in the absence of a member of the nonpolitical staff.[43] While this

---

[41] See, for example, testimony of John W. Dean III, *Select Committee Hearings*, Phase I, Book 3, pp. 942-945, particularly the following passage from pp. 944-945:

"And I will begin by summarizing and saying to the best of my recollection it was in early July when I called Gray to discuss the matter of receiving reports from the FBI. Gray indicated that he was going to be in his office on Saturday and that I should come to his office and take a look at the reports in his office. I told him that I thought it was unwise for me to be coming in and out of the Justice Department, particularly since most of the guards and people at the Justice Department knew me. Accordingly, we arranged to meet later at his apartment and he said that he would discuss the matter with me then. I recall we took a stroll to the side of his apartment building and sat on a bench in front of the river and talked generally about the case and I raised with him the matter of my receiving some of the raw FBI data regarding the investigation. Gray said that he would have to check but wanted an assurance from me that this information was being reported to the President and that was the principal purpose of the request. I assured him that it was being reported to the President. Even though I was not directly reporting to the President at that time. I was aware of the fact that Ehrlichman or Haldeman had daily discussions with the President, and I felt certain, because Haldeman often made notes of my reporting back about the information I was bringing to their attention, that this information was being given to the President.

"I do not recall when actually I received the first written information from the FBI, but I believe it was after July 21 when I received a summary report that had been prepared on the investigation to that stage."

[42] Thomas Griffith, "Putting Politics in Its Place at the Justice Department," *Fortune*, October 1973, p. 228.

[43] The practice of Louis Oberdorfer of not seeing anyone who might be involved in litigation (reported in ibid.), while commendable, seems unrealistic when ap-

would raise problems as a universal practice (for example, negotiations with Mr. Agnew's lawyers), the fact that it was the normal routine would deter those with improper motives. Consideration might also be given to "contracting out" large areas of litigation to private lawyers. While ultimate control of the disposition of cases must continue to rest in the Department of Justice, the presence of outside lawyers on a case would be a strong deterrent to improper influence. There are dangers, however. The fees involved might well be sufficiently attractive to make the contracting out of cases a form of patronage and the lawyers hired might thus be partisan themselves.

A similar approach might be used in other agencies although no detailed analysis will be made here. For example, while tax policy must be subject to political control, tax returns might be under the control of an independent repository and available only on certain specified conditions.

Special Prosecutors. The investigation and prosecution of crimes committed by officials of the executive branch or by their political opponents is a long standing problem, brought into focus once more by Watergate. For many reasons an independent prosecutor is desirable in most such cases. One reason is the conflict of interest inherent in Department of Justice lawyers conducting the investigation. There is the inevitable danger of improper influence and the destruction or neglect of evidence. Even in honestly conducted investigations, however, those charged with the inquiry are necessarily in a difficult situation, since they must investigate criminal charges in which those who have considerable power over their futures have a personal interest. And, even the most honest and unhampered investigation may create public suspicion if subject to control by persons directly involved.

Another reason is that witnesses may be afraid to tell their stories candidly where the investigator or prosecutor is from the Department of Justice, for fear their testimony will be reported to those being investigated.

Finally there is the legal issue of the justiciability of the use of compulsory process against the President by a prosecutor subject to his authority. Because the litigant seeking the subpoena is subordinate

---

(Footnote 43 continued)
plied to every non-career department official. Approaches will be made, and may even be useful to the department. Suggesting that a career attorney be present lessens the possibility of blatantly improper approaches, while preserving any beneficial results that may accrue. Additionally, heavy penalties for not following the suggested formula will be a sufficient deterrent to attempts at corruption.

to the person against whom it is directed and can be ordered on pain of discharge to cease the litigation, the case might be treated as a request for an advisory opinion from the courts and a "family quarrel" resolvable solely within the executive branch.[44]

Similar considerations apply to investigations of members of the opposition party for violations of federal election laws. Here also the likelihood of a conflict of interest, the danger of harassment, and the fear of witnesses may exist. The urge to regulate elections generated by Watergate has made consideration of some such mechanism imperative.

The need for a permanent independent prosecutorial office has not been established. In more tranquil times, it would have little to do. What is needed is legislative provision for the judicial appointment of a special counsel to particular grand juries, the counsel to be independent of control by the Department of Justice. The decision as to whether the need for a special counsel exists ought not be made by the political branches as each case arises. Leaving these responsibilities to the various district courts thus seems the best solution.[45]

The very existence of this standing mechanism would tend to provide a deterrent to the use of improper influence in criminal investigations. One may speculate as to different courses the Watergate affair might have taken had such a mechanism existed. The Justice Department itself might find the mechanism useful, moreover, inasmuch as resort to ad hoc special investigators or prosecutors has had a stormy history. Both Newbold Morris in the Truman administration[46] and Archibald Cox in more recent times[47] became embroiled in disputes which led to their dismissal. When the appointing agency is the Department of Justice, it alone can determine the prosecutor's or investigator's jurisdiction and powers and must be the ultimate arbiter in disputes over them. But the investigator or prosecutor inevitably feels that his "independence" calls for resistance to instructions from the department. Where a judge makes the appointment and defines

---

[44] Alexander M. Bickel, "The Tapes, Cox, Nixon," *The New Republic*, September 29, 1973, p. 13.

[45] Bills to create such temporary offices have been introduced, among them S. 2642 (introduced by Sen. Taft), S. 2611 (introduced by Sen. Bayh), S. 2603 (introduced by Sen. Stevenson), and S. 2616 (introduced by Sen. Percy), all 93rd Congress, 1st session.

[46] For capsule explanations of the controversy, see two newspaper articles by Arthur Krock, "Truman Dismissed McGrath After Opposing Both Morris and Income Questionnaires," *New York Times*, April 6, 1952, p. 1, col. 1, and "McGrath Cleared Ouster of Morris," *New York Times*, April 9, 1952, p. 18, col. 3.

[47] See *Hearings on the Special Prosecutor before the Committee on the Judiciary, United States Senate*, 93rd Congress, 1st session (1973).

the jurisdiction and powers, subsequent disputes can be resolved by the court, or through settlement, without the fear that independence will be compromised.

The objections to such a proposal are of two sorts—one going to its wisdom, the other to its constitutionality. This issue might, after all, also be left largely to the political process. Recent history does demonstrate that a most reluctant administration can be compelled by political considerations alone to appoint a special prosecutor. The issue is one of balancing costs against anticipated benefits. The existence of a standing mechanism may have a deterrent as well as remedial effect, and the fact that special prosecutors have sometimes been appointed is no answer to the suggestion that inadequate investigations can thwart the development of political pressure. Still, there is room for disagreement.

Another prudential demurrer is that decisions to investigate and prosecute ought to be subject to political control, a point strengthened by the way in which the Agnew case was disposed of. As a general rule this proposition is true, for general policies can be executed only in particular cases. The Agnew case may be exceptional, however, and the kinds of crimes most likely to call for an independent prosecutor do not normally entail major policy questions. The prosecution of officials for obstruction of justice, bribery, and the like is not an issue of the same dimensions as a decision to put more resources in the fight for civil rights or the fight against organized crime. Major policy issues will, on the other hand, arise in cases involving violation of election laws, whether by supporters of the incumbents or by the opposition. The risks in election cases are even greater, but safeguards can be established.

The real danger is that several hundred district judges would attain a degree of control over the prosecutorial machinery through this device and might abuse it. In *United States* v. *Cox*, for example, a district judge for the District of Mississippi sought (and was reversed on appeal) [48] to hold a United States attorney in contempt for failing to prosecute civil rights advocates for perjury.

There are risks, therefore, in the Justice Department's surrendering its authority to decline to prosecute, but retention of this power can be accommodated to the proposal. A special counsel can have authority to issue compulsory process, grant immunity, and otherwise assist and direct a grand jury without control by the Department of Justice. The rule that the United States attorney must sign an indict-

---

[48] United States v. Cox, 342 F. 2d 167 (5th Cir., 1965), cert. den. sub. nom. Cox v. Hauberg, 381 U.S. 935.

ment [49] may be retained, and the special counsel will become a special prosecutor upon obtaining the signature. If the United States attorney declines to sign, the statute might provide that the grand jury's presentment be publicized in the discretion of the judge. The United States attorney might also be required to state the reasons why the Justice Department was not proceeding with the case. This sort of arrangement avoids both the dangers of *Cox* and the dangers of Watergate: a heavy political price will be paid for failure to prosecute where there is a strong case.

Where the grand jury declines to indict, however, the United States attorney would be powerless to compel it to do so. There might also be a provision for an expedited appeal by the Department of Justice if it objects to the appointment of a special counsel, a provision that would also serve to prevent abuses by district judges.

Another objection is that the judge who appoints a special counsel may not be able to sit impartially on cases or motions the counsel may argue. This problem, if it is a problem, might be avoided by the judge's recusing himself after naming the special prosecutor, or by lodging the appointment itself, upon the judge's finding that special counsel should be appointed, in another judge or in the judicial council for the circuit. Finally, administrative arrangements providing funds to carry on independent investigations would avoid total reliance upon the Department of Justice for investigatory resources.

The basic constitutional objection is that the power to prosecute is vested exclusively in the President (and the executive branch) by Article II which empowers him "to take Care that the Laws be faithfully executed." Some judicial decisions seem to support this view. In *Cox*, the court of appeals' reversal of the district court held that prosecution is an executive function to be exercised according to executive discretion and free from judicial interference.[50] Similarly, in *Nader* v. *Bork*,[51] Judge Gesell indicated by way of dictum that conferring the power to appoint a special independent prosecutor upon the courts would place incompatible (and presumably unconstitutional) duties upon them.[52] Finally, *United States* v. *Solomon*[53] held that the statutory power of courts to name temporary United States

---

[49] Rule 7(c), Federal Rules of Criminal Procedure.

[50] 342 F. 2d 167 (5th Cir., 1965).

[51] Civil Action No. 1954-73 (D.D.C., 1973), reprinted in *Hearings on the Special Prosecutor before the Committee on the Judiciary, United States Senate*, 93rd Congress, 1st session (1973), Part II, p. 480.

[52] Ibid., p. 484.

[53] 216 F. Supp. 835 (S.D.N.Y., 1963).

attorneys pending a permanent appointment was constitutional. The theory of the opinion, however, strongly suggests that only temporary appointments subject to presidential revocation are proper.

These cases are not conclusive. *Cox*, for example, actually involves the question of whether there is inherent judicial power to compel prosecution, a question quite different from the one now under discussion. Judge Gesell's remarks in *Nader* were gratuitous dicta, and the *Solomon* decision can be read considerably more narrowly.

Many authorities look in the other direction. Article II empowers Congress to vest the courts with power to appoint inferior federal officers.[54] If notions of separation of powers have any validity, this power is surely limited. Congress cannot, for example, vest the district court for the District of Columbia with power to appoint the secretary of state. A sensible limitation consistent with notions of separation of powers is that offices which courts may constitutionally fill must somehow be connected with the judicial branch or the judicial function.[55]

In *ex parte Siebold*, the Supreme Court upheld the power of Congress to vest in the federal courts appointment of supervisors of elections for national offices.[56] On this issue the Court said that

> It is no doubt usual and proper to vest the appointment of inferior officers in that department of the government, executive or judicial, or in that particular executive department to which the duties of such officers appertain. But there is no absolute requirement to this effect in the Constitution; and if there were, it would be difficult in many cases to determine to which department an office properly belonged. . . .
>
> But as the Constitution stands, the selection of the appointing power, as between the functionaries named, is a matter resting in the discretion of Congress.[57]

The court went on to suggest that there might be such an "incongruity in the duty required as to excuse the courts from its per-

---

[54] U.S. Constitution, Article II, Section 2:
 ". . . the Congress may by law vest the Appointment of such inferior Officers, as they think proper, in the President alone, in the Courts of Law, or in the Heads of Departments."

[55] See, for example, testimony of Philip B. Kurland, *Hearings on the Special Prosecutor before the Committee on the Judiciary, United States Senate*, 93rd Congress, 1st session (1973), Part 1, pp. 321-323.

[56] 100 U.S. 371 (1879).

[57] Ibid., pp. 397-398.

formance. . . ." [58] No such incongruity exists in the appointment of special counsel to grand juries, for such counsel are intimately related to the judicial function, the grand jury itself being part of the judicial branch.

Lower court decisions also support the view that vesting such appointment power in the judiciary is constitutionally valid. For example, it has been held that the courts may even appoint members of the District of Columbia school board,[59] and there are now several cases in which officials of the government have been forced to initiate various kinds of legal actions.[60]

The appointment of counsel in particular cases is a longstanding judicial function.[61] Historically, there has never been the rigid separation of powers implied by those who view the proposal as unconstitutional. The grand jury in many states has considerable independent power.[62] And in Connecticut, for example, prosecutors are appointed by the courts in which they serve.[63]

Of course, if judges have the power to appoint, they also have the power to remove the special counsel,[64] presumably under the standards governing removal of a special defense counsel. This seems to pose no particular difficulty.

The Select Committee ought to recommend, therefore, that when a district court has found that there is probable cause to believe a crime has been committed, that an investigation and prosecution by the Department of Justice might entail a conflict of interest, that persons under investigation are high level officials of the government, that witnesses may fear to testify before regular employees of the Department of Justice, that a question of justiciability as to a subpoena may be raised, or that a violation of federal election laws

---

[58] Ibid., p. 398.

[59] Hobson v. Hansen, 265 F. Supp. 902 (D.D.C., 1967).

[60] See, for example, De Vito v. Shultz, 300 F. Supp. 381 (D.D.C., 1969), Adams v. Richardson, Civ. No. 3095-70 (D.D.C., November 16, 1972), and Joint Tribal Council of the Passamaquoddy Tribe v. Morton, Civ. No. 1960 (D.Me., filed June 2, 1972).

[61] Federal judges have long appointed counsel for indigent criminal defendants. For a discussion of common law precedent and statutory authorization in state courts, see "Note, The Special Prosecutor in the Federal System: A Proposal," *American Criminal Law Review*, vol. 11 (1973), pp. 578-586.

[62] Ibid.

[63] 51 *Conn. Gen. Stats.*, Section 175.

[64] See, for example, Shurtleff v. United States, 189 U.S. 311 (1903), holding that the right to appoint engenders a comparable right to remove (absent an express bar on the right of removal).

may be involved, the court may in its discretion appoint a special counsel to the grand jury. Such a special counsel would have power to pursue the investigation unhindered, but indictments would depend upon approval of the Department of Justice. If the department refused to proceed, it would have to state its reasons. The judge might then, in his discretion, order that the presentment become a matter of public record.

Watergate and the Power of the Presidency

At a time when concern is widely expressed that the presidency has become too powerful, the Watergate affair has added fuel to an established fire. The conclusion that excessive presidential power and Watergate are related, however, is not self-evident. A President with even modest powers might nevertheless act illegally against his political opponents. To weaken the presidency to the point that such activities could not occur would disable it from doing anything else. Two specific aspects of the office may be said to have contributed to Watergate and related events. First, access to manpower and technology facilitated the break-in.[65] The President, however, has no

---

[65] See, for example, testimony of John W. Dean III, *Select Committee Hearings*, Phase I, Book 3, pp. 919-926, detailing White House efforts to curtail "leaks," to gather "political intelligence," and to create "Operation Sandwedge." Although the funding for these operations was presumably to come from nongovernment sources, the men involved were federal employees, concocting these schemes while on the government payroll. See also testimony of John Ehrlichman in ibid., Phase I, Book 6, pp. 2530-2531.

"The Attorney General then reported in response to an inquiry, and maybe I had better tell you how the inquiry came up. Mr. Krogh came to me and said, 'I am having real trouble getting the FBI to move on this.' And so I said 'Well' and basically my function was to do downfield blocking for Mr. Krogh when he had problems in the Department. I said 'OK, I will contact the Attorney General and see what I can do,' which I did. The Attorney called me back and he said: 'We have a very tough problem here. It appears that a top man in the FBI put in a routine request that Mr. Ellsberg's father-in-law be interviewed. The Director has given that top man notice that he is going to be transferred and demoted, and he has further given notice that that interview and interviews of that family are not to take place.'

"Now this was the area in which Mr. Krogh and the special unit were pressing for the Department of Justice to bring information together as was their job to do. The Attorney General said, 'I am going to reverse this decision on the part of the Director to transfer this man and demote him' but he said 'We have a very touchy situation with the Director. Mr. Sullivan in the Bureau is extremely upset and concerned and disagrees strongly with the Director in this matter, I don't know but what Mr. Sullivan may quit as a result of this whole episode, it's very touchy within the Bureau.' I said, 'What are our chances of getting the Bureau to move ahead on this right away,' and he said, 'Very slim or none.'

monopoly of these resources. Second, presidential regulatory power created the opportunity to pressure firms and individuals for money.[66]

Many of the proposals bruited about these days are a bit beside the point. They aim only at a general weakening of the presidency rather than at the specific aspects of the presidential office which contributed to Watergate. They do not, therefore, require more than cursory discussion, and that only because they have received recent attention. One suggestion is that the presidential power be exercised by a committee, a proposal designed to eliminate the entrusting of such awesome power to one man.[67] Destroying the unity of the office would do more than lead to shared responsibility, however: it would also disable the office from performing those functions for which unity seems necessary. The question repeated every day by representatives of foreign nations—What is American policy toward this country or that?—can never be confidently answered if the ultimate policy making authority is a committee governed by shifting coalitions. Most policy issues, moreover, involve a choice among many options; a committee might be able to decide only on maintenance of the status quo, and that by default. Important foreign policy decisions ought not be made on a series of four-to-three votes, thus weakening the force of the decisions themselves and tempting other nations to play for the vote of one person. Similar considerations are true of virtually all executive decisions whether they be appointments, prosecutions or domestic policy. A cabinet reflecting the views of a badly divided presidential committee does not seem possible. And, if we are concerned about unscrupulousness in the presidency, a committee structure would only encourage bargaining and wheeling and dealing.

The committee proposal is in some ways a straw man but the suggestion that Presidents be limited to one six-year term has been

---

(Footnote 65 continued)

"So it was very—this set of facts, and the real strong feeling of the President that there was a legitimate and vital national security aspect to this, that it was decided, first on Mr. Krogh's recommendation, with my concurrence, that the two men in this special unit who had had considerable investigative experience, be assigned to follow up on the then leads and rather general leads which were in the file."

[66] See, for example, statement by Senator Ervin, in *Select Committee Hearings* (mimeo.), vol. 52, p. 10060.

[67] Barbara Tuchman, "Should We Abolish the Presidency?" *New York Times*, February 13, 1973. For a variation on this theme, see Max Lerner, "Presidential Watchman," *New York Post*, June 11, 1972.

more seriously made.[68] To the extent such a proposal seeks support in Watergate, it is an overreaction. To be sure, a President running for reelection may be tempted to resort to illegal tactics, but so may a retiring President desiring to be succeeded by a member of his own party. The proposal, moreover, would seem to weaken the President where the cooperation of other branches is necessary (as, for example, in legislation) by establishing him as "lame duck" at the beginning of his term. At the same time, it would encourage unilateral action without regard either to public opinion or to the Congress, where he has independent power. It may well be that presidential decisions to use force in foreign affairs, for instance, would be more, rather than less, likely under such a structure.

Finally, there are a number of suggestions for change in the direction of a parliamentary model.[69] One danger here is the elimination of the power of the political executive while the weaknesses of the Congress persist, as in the Fourth French Republic.[70] Alternatively, effective parliamentary rule, as in Great Britain, entails far more centralized power in one political leader than does our presidential system.[71] It is uncertain, given our present state of knowledge, in which direction the shift would occur, which is reason enough to stay the hand of hasty reform.

Much of the concern over the power of the presidency and many of the allegations on Watergate mistake the source of much presidential power. Most decidedly it is not derived solely from Article II of the Constitution which empowers the President to "take Care that the Laws be faithfully executed," serve as commander-in-chief of the armed forces, deliver information to Congress on the state of the union, call special sessions of Congress, make appointments with the advice and consent of the Senate, receive ambassadors, grant pardons and veto congressional legislation subject to being overridden by a two-thirds vote.[72]

---

[68] See "Single Six-Year Term for President," *Hearings before the Judiciary Committee of the House of Representatives*, 92nd Congress, 1st session (1971); Arthur M. Schlesinger, Jr. and Alfred de Grazia, *Congress and the Presidency: Their Role in Modern Times* (Washington, D. C.: American Enterprise Institute, 1967). See also Arthur M. Schlesinger, Jr., *The Imperial Presidency*.

[69] See, for example, E. S. Corwin, *The President: Office and Powers* (New York: New York University Press, 1957), p. 296.

[70] See generally, Philip M. Williams, *Crisis and Compromise: Politics in the Fourth Republic* (Hamden, Conn.: Archon Books, 1964).

[71] Richard Rose, *Politics In England: An Interpretation* (Boston: Little, Brown & Co., 1964), p. 193.

[72] U.S. Constitution, Article II, Sections 2-3.

Actual presidential power far exceeds the powers enumerated in that catalog,[73] largely because of increased American involvement in foreign affairs and congressional action which has enormously strengthened the presidency. With the President's primacy in foreign policy,[74] increasing world involvement has necessarily increased presidential power. He commands armed forces of two to three million men, directs sophisticated intelligence agencies and holds ultimate authority over weapons which can destroy the world. Such power generates further power by creating around the President the mystique of the man with the "button."

The increasing complexity of governmental responsibility, moreover, gives the presidency considerable power over public opinion. His proposals almost always are spotlighted for the public and thus receive great attention, while proposals emanating from Congress necessarily seem conflicting and confusing.

As important is the legal power of the President in domestic affairs, power which is in almost every case directly traceable to the Congress.[75] The President appoints members of regulatory agencies to which Congress has delegated power over the economy, and he himself has been given considerable regulatory discretion. He can, for example, set milk price supports, fix all wages and prices, and will soon have virtually unlimited discretion over the allocation of energy. Such enormous power necessarily gives a President "muscle" with businessmen, farm groups, and unions.

He has corresponding powers where politicians are concerned. Grants for urban renewal, manpower training, federal construction,

---

[73] For discussions of presidential power, see Clinton Rossiter, *The American Presidency* (New York: Harcourt, Brace & World, Inc., 1960); Wilfred E. Binkley, *The Man in the White House* (Baltimore: Johns Hopkins Press, 1958); James MacGregor Burns, *Presidential Government* (Boston: Houghton-Mifflin Co., 1973); George E. Reedy, *The Twilight of the Presidency* (New York: World Publishing Co., 1970); Richard E. Neustadt, *Presidential Power* (New York: John Wiley & Sons, Inc., 1960); Emmet John Hughes, *The Living Presidency* (New York: Coward, McCann & Geoghegan, Inc., 1973); Arthur M. Schlesinger, Jr. and Alfred de Grazia, *Congress and the Presidency: Their Role in Modern Times*.

[74] The Supreme Court has characterized this as "the very delicate, plenary and exclusive power of the President as the sole organ of the federal government in the field of international relations," United States v. Curtiss-Wright Export Corp., 299 U.S. 304, 320 (1936). See Louis Henkin, *Foreign Affairs and the Constitution* (Mineola, N.Y.: Foundation Press, 1972), pp. 37-64. But see, Charles A. Lofgren, "United States v. Curtiss-Wright Corporation: An Historical Reassessment," *Yale Law Journal*, vol. 83 (1973), p. 1.

[75] See, for example, the remark by Senator Ervin that it is Congress that is "the chief aggrandizer of the Executive," *Congressional Record*, June 4, 1973, S. 10235-10236.

poverty programs, model cities, and so on ad infinitum, obviously are of value to congressmen as well as to state and local officials, and it is impossible to detect all but gross political distortions in their allocation.

The net result is that Congress has delegated enormous authority easily translatable into raw political power. The possibility of direct abuse is always present and likely can be found in every administration. The total impact of this power may, however, be subtle.

The President's domestic power is such that citizens and politically active groups increasingly view their stake in the presidency less in terms of national issues of general importance, and more in terms of obtaining specific action on behalf of narrow economic or political interests. This in turn increases presidential power over issues of national concern. If one's immediate and specific concern in the presidency is an increase in price support levels, seeing an agreeable appointment to a regulatory agency, or getting an urban renewal grant to administer, one's lobbying is hardly likely to be accompanied by adverse comments on the President's foreign policy. The total power delegated by the Congress to the President may thus exceed the sum of its component parts.

If Congress is seriously concerned about presidential power, it should refrain from increasing it through domestic legislation before it turns to radical institutional rearrangements. The legislative routine should include an assessment of the effect on presidential power of all proposed legislation. For example, the Kennedy-Scott proposal to subsidize presidential campaigns and eliminate private financing should be viewed as legislation which will increase the power of incumbent presidents eligible for reelection. For whereas any challenger will be limited to the modest resources provided by government, a sitting President has ample opportunity to campaign through "nonpolitical" activities.[76] Establishing such a routine will not be easy, however, for many of the congressmen who are apprehensive at presidential power are fervent advocates of measures which increase it.

If Congress's obvious first step is to refrain from further strengthening of the presidency, its second is to strengthen itself. Notions of separation of powers call for mutual strength rather than mutual weakness. Two branches of government seeking to weaken each other institutionally can only decrease the quality of government. Two strong branches functioning efficiently within their areas of

---

[76] See notes 59 and 60, Chapter 1, and accompanying text.

responsibility can provide statesmanlike governance and yet protect against the excessive concentration of power.[77] Instead of weakening the presidency by imposing institutional restraints, Congress should arrange itself so as to recapture control of the budgeting process [78] and play a role in establishing overall foreign policy goals. It is not the lack of suggestions for steps in this direction but congressional reluctance which bars the way. For Congress can reduce the relative power of the presidency simply by fulfilling its own responsibilities.

For all its rhetoric about presidential usurpation, Congress has been too willing to leave responsibility to the President. That the initiative for most important legislation rests with the executive branch rather than the Congress indicates where the will and the resources to lead now abide. It is only a change in will, a change in Congress's view of itself, coupled with technical changes to increase congressional ability to act, that will alter the present pattern of legislative ennui.

Much of the impoundment controversy, for example, bespeaks a congressional desire to approve spending programs while relying on presidential impoundment to avoid tax increases.[79] Similarly, Congress for years declared neither peace nor war in Vietnam, but instead delegated de facto—many said de jure—power to do either to the President.

Congress should react negatively to exercises of power by the President which intrude on legislative functions, regardless of what political interests are furthered. Quite the opposite usually happens. Those who would most quickly praise or condemn the use of executive orders in the area of civil rights are often the quickest to condemn or praise it in the area of domestic subversion.[80] Congress must in short transcend the immediate policy issues and act out of an institu-

---

[77] See *The Federalist*, numbers 48 and 51.

[78] For one suggestion of how this could occur, see Aaron B. Wildavsky, "The Annual Expenditure Increment—or How Congress Can Regain Control of the Budget," *The Public Interest*, no. 33 (Fall 1973), p. 84. See also Murray L. Weidenbaum, Dan Larkins, and Philip N. Marcus, *Matching Needs and Resources: Reforming the Federal Budget* (Washington, D. C.: American Enterprise Institute, 1973). And see generally, Alfred de Grazia et al., *Congress: The First Branch of Government* (Washington, D. C.: American Enterprise Institute, 1966).

[79] See Wildavsky, "The Annual Expenditure Increment."

[80] See generally, *Hearings on the Philadelphia Plan before the Subcommittee on Separation of Powers of the Committee on the Judiciary, United States Senate,* 91st Congress, 1st session (1969), and *Hearings on S. 2466 and S. Res. 163 before the Subcommittee on Separation of Powers of the Committee on the Judiciary, United States Senate,* 92nd Congress, 1st session (1971).

tional sense when addressing exercises of power by the President which intrude on the legislative function. Proposals to democratize the operations of the House and Senate may in this sense be counter-productive, for they tend to deprive the leadership of a stake in the institution and increase its need to respond to immediate political considerations. Gains in the area of separation of powers may thus be made only at a temporary cost in immediate policy results.

CONCLUSIONS

The problem of preventing future Watergates cannot be fully resolved by law. If law alone were enough, after all, there would have been no Watergate to begin with, for there are laws aplenty against such ventures.

The place at which sensible reform begins is acceptance of the fact that no law will stop men with a strong will to disregard it. Accepting this casts doubt on the need for radical reform of existing legal and institutional arrangements. The existing structure may in fact have contributed little to the events of Watergate. The goal for which we must strive is a legal structure which will require even stronger will on the part of those who would violate it for political purposes. This, however, calls for a careful tailoring of remedies rather than a wholesale rearranging of our institutions.

The Watergate participants may have fallen too easily into their schemes because the lower echelons expected protection by the higher-ups, while they in turn apparently thought their control of the machinery of government was protection enough. This is a problem of crime detection, not the wholesale corruption of the political process; and it calls for remedies tailored to the demonstrated imperfections rather than expansive changes in the structure of the executive branch.

Similarly, abuses of the power to act in the interests of national security call for raising the political cost of excessive conduct rather than for attempts to outlaw practices characteristic of major governments. Watergate showed in part that the failure precisely to locate authority for such actions in accountable officials increases the risks of abuse. The failure tends to spread that authority too thinly and reduces the perceived political cost by creating the expectation that misadventures can be disavowed. Locating sole authority in a designated and accountable official (for example, the President) is no guarantee against excessive acts but it raises the political risk sufficiently to ensure genuinely careful consideration of the need for such actions.

Because so much depends on imposing high political as well as legal penalties on official miscreants, one aspect of the Select Committee's investigation is disquieting. The Senate restricted the committee to the 1972 election, thus excluding campaigns of equal relevance to its legislative purpose but which occurred while Democrats controlled the White House. Whatever reason the Senate may have had, the belief that vigorous investigations will be restricted to the conduct of the opposition party cannot be eliminated.

Nothing in Watergate calls for major tampering with the political process. Both the calls for an end to private campaign financing and the suggestions for institutional changes in the presidency may result more from the fact that these were preexisting goals of many of the political beneficiaries of Watergate than from any connection with the affair itself. Regulation of campaign financing seems bound to limit political freedom and increase the hold of incumbents on their offices, a most ironic "reform" to come out of a scandal that involved political espionage and sabotage by government officials. The irony is underlined by the fact that all the proposals include limitations on expenditures by candidates, a provision attacked as unconstitutional by leading constitutional scholars [1] and held a prior restraint on the press by a lower court in the District of Columbia.[2] Suggestions that Congress rush headlong into "reforms" which so many believe violate First Amendment rights vividly demonstrates the risk of misunderstanding the lessons of Watergate.

Reduction of presidential power, on the other hand, is more a question of Congress reforming itself and accepting responsibility for governing than of institutionally damaging the executive branch. The suggestion that the executive become a committee of six is little more than an example of how bizarre proposals emanating from Watergate can be while the single six-year term seems unwise as well as unrelated to the affair.

If the most talked about "reforms" are adopted, the judgment of history is likely to be that one real disaster of Watergate was "[summing] it so well that it came to far more than the Witnesses

---

[1] See note 8, Introduction, *supra.;* notes 44 and 45, Chapter 1, *supra.*

[2] See note 46, Chapter 1, *supra.*

ever had said!"[3] The lessons of Watergate are incremental and so are the true reforms which should come out of it. Radical alterations in the political process are steps into the unknown which are quite as likely to bring about a relapse as to effect a cure. Consider the impact of the Kennedy-Scott proposal on the power of an incumbent President eligible for reelection.[4] Consider how the reporting provisions of the Federal Election Campaign Act of 1971 made the centralized financing of the Committee to Re-Elect the President inevitable.[5] Both, however, are pressed as "reforms" which will in one fashion or another cleanse the political process. If the lessons of Watergate continue to be misunderstood, all that is certain is that more truly catastrophic effects are yet to come.

---

[3] Lewis Carroll, *The Hunting of the Snark: The Barrister's Dream* (New York: Pantheon, 1966).

[4] See note 59, Chapter 1, *supra*.

[5] Herbert E. Alexander, "Impact of New Federal Election Laws in the United States," paper delivered to the International Political Science Association Congress, August 22, 1973, p. 20.